PC Magazine
Guide to Windows
for Workgroups

PC Magazine Guide to Windows for Workgroups

Frank J. Derfler, Jr., and Les Freed

Ziff-Davis Press
Emeryville, California

Development Editor	Eric Stone
Copy Editors	Noelle Graney and Melinda Levine
Technical Reviewer	The LeBlond Group
Project Coordinator	Ami Knox
Proofreaders	Janna Hecker Clark and Vanessa Miller
Cover Design	Kenneth Roberts and Carrie English
Cover Illustration	Carrie English
Book Design	Paper Crane Graphics, Berkeley
Technical Illustration	Cherie Plumlee Computer Graphics & Illustration
Word Processing	Howard Blechman and Cat Haglund
Page Layout	M. D. Barrera
Indexer	Valerie Haynes Perry

This book was produced on a Macintosh IIfx, with the following applications: FrameMaker®, Microsoft® Word, MacLink®Plus, Aldus® FreeHand™, Adobe Photoshop™, and Collage Plus™.

Ziff-Davis Press
5903 Christie Avenue
Emeryville, CA 94608

Copyright © 1993 by Ziff-Davis Press. All rights reserved.

PC Magazine is a registered trademark of Ziff Communications Company. Ziff-Davis Press, ZD Press, and PC Magazine Guide To are trademarks of Ziff Communications Company.

All other product names and services identified throughout this book are trademarks or registered trademarks of their respective companies. They are used throughout this book in editorial fashion only and for the benefit of such companies. No such uses, or the use of any trade name, is intended to convey endorsement or other affiliation with the book.

No part of this publication may be reproduced in any form, or stored in a database or retrieval system, or transmitted or distributed in any form by any means, electronic, mechanical photocopying, recording, or otherwise, without the prior written permission of Ziff-Davis Press, except as permitted by the Copyright Act of 1976 and except that program listings may be entered, stored, and executed in a computer system.

THE INFORMATION AND MATERIAL CONTAINED IN THIS BOOK ARE PROVIDED "AS IS," WITHOUT WARRANTY OF ANY KIND, EXPRESS OR IMPLIED, INCLUDING WITHOUT LIMITATION ANY WARRANTY CONCERNING THE ACCURACY, ADEQUACY, OR COMPLETENESS OF SUCH INFORMATION OR MATERIAL OR THE RESULTS TO BE OBTAINED FROM USING SUCH INFORMATION OR MATERIAL. NEITHER ZIFF-DAVIS PRESS NOR THE AUTHOR SHALL BE RESPONSIBLE FOR ANY CLAIMS ATTRIBUTABLE TO ERRORS, OMISSIONS, OR OTHER INACCURACIES IN THE INFORMATION OR MATERIAL CONTAINED IN THIS BOOK, AND IN NO EVENT SHALL ZIFF-DAVIS PRESS OR THE AUTHOR BE LIABLE FOR DIRECT, INDIRECT, SPECIAL, INCIDENTAL, OR CONSEQUENTIAL DAMAGES ARISING OUT OF THE USE OF SUCH INFORMATION OR MATERIAL.

ISBN 1-56276-120-X

Manufactured in the United States of America
 ⊕ The paper used in this book exceeds the EPA requirements for postconsumer recycled paper.
10 9 8 7 6 5 4 3 2 1

■ Contents at a Glance

Introduction		XV
Chapter 1:	Networking under Windows for Workgroups	1
Chapter 2:	Planning Your Network	17
Chapter 3:	Installing Windows for Workgroups	33
Chapter 4:	Windows for Workgroups Basics	45
Chapter 5:	Using the Electronic Mail	63
Chapter 6:	The First Forms Program: Schedule+	83
Chapter 7:	Using Windows for Workgroups with Other Networks	101
Chapter 8:	Applications and Windows for Workgroups	121
Chapter 9:	Network Communications	147
Chapter 10:	The Workgroup Connection	163
Chapter 11:	Fine-Tuning Windows for Workgroups	183
Appendix:	The Hearts Game: Network Fun!	197
Glossary		200
Index		207

■ Table of Contents

Introduction	XV

Chapter 1: Networking under Windows for Workgroups — 1

The Windows Family — 3
    Better Than NT? 3
    Mail and Scheduling 5
    Networked Dynamic Data Exchange (DDE) 6

Benefits for NetWare Users — 8

Installation Overview — 8

How Much Horsepower? — 10

Other Servers — 10

Weaving It All Together — 12

The Universal Client — 14

Chapter 2: Planning Your Network — 17

Taking an Inventory — 18

Defining Your Requirements — 20

Core Planning Issues — 22
    Crossing Adapters and Cabling 22
    Server Requirements 25
    Those Darn Printers 27

Additional Planning Factors — 27
    The Server Directory Structure 28
    Menu Systems 28

Network Security 29
Backup 29
Training 30

Chapter 3: Installing Windows for Workgroups — 33

Hardware Installation — 34

Finding a Home for Your NIC Board 34
Understanding I/O and Memory Addressing 36
Selecting Interrupt Request (IRQ) Lines 37
Selecting an I/O and Memory Address 37

Windows for Workgroups Installation — 38

Installing Windows for Workgroups on Your Local Hard Disk 40
Installing Windows for Workgroups from a File Server 40
Windows for Workgroups, CONFIG.SYS, and AUTOEXEC.BAT 41
When Things Go Wrong . . . 42

Chapter 4: Windows for Workgroups Basics — 45

So What Does It Do? — 46

Using and Sharing Disks and Printers — 48

Using a Shared Disk 48
Sharing Your Disk 51
Sharing Printers 53

Using the Chat Program — 60

Network Etiquette — 61

Chapter 5: Using the Electronic Mail — 63

Electronic Mail as a Workgroup Productivity Tool — 64

Electronic Mail Program Functions — 65

The Concept	65
Installing Mail	66
Placing the .MMF File	69
Specifying Notification of Messages	71
Making Mail	71
Addressing a Message 72	
Mailing from the File Manager 74	
Preparing the Text 75	
Putting Pictures in the Text 76	
Sending It Off 77	
Managing the Incoming Mail	77
Sharing Folders 79	
Finding Messages 80	
Managing the Mail System	80

Chapter 6: The First Forms Program: Schedule+ 83

Forms Handling	84
Schedule+ Basics	85
Presentations and Views 86	
Invitations and Confirmations 86	
User Names 87	
Scheduling of Shared Resources 87	
Distribution Lists 88	
Holidays 89	
Tasks 89	
Notes and To-Do Lists 90	
Meeting Times 91	
Access rights 91	
Recurring Events 92	
Printed Calendars 92	
Searches 93	

A Few Tips 93
Set the Meeting with the Mouse 94
Drag and Drop Tasks 94
Click on the Busy Bar 97
Set Access Privileges 97

Chapter 7: Using Windows for Workgroups with Other Networks 101

Who Needs a Server, Anyway? 102

Using NetWare with Windows for Workgroups 104
The NetWare DOS Client Software 104
Installing NetWare Support in Windows for Workgroups 105
Controlling NetWare from Windows 109
Using NetWare Printers 113

Using LAN Manager with Windows for Workgroups 114
Preparing to Use LAN Manager 114
Using LAN Manager Drives and Printers 115

Sharing Files and Printers with Macintosh Computers 115
Putting Macs on the Network 116
Whose File Is This? 117
Sharing Printers 118

Chapter 8: Applications and Windows for Workgroups 121

Windows × LANs × Applications = Challenge 122
Our Best Advice 123
No Floppy Drives 125
Easy Installation 126
Using Files on the Network 127
Sharing Printers 129

Microsoft Word 2.0 and Excel 4.0	130
Microsoft PowerPoint Version 3.0	132
Lotus 1-2-3 for Windows and Ami Pro	133
WordPerfect for Windows	135
Networked DDE: A Tutorial	137
Clipboards and ClipBooks 138	
Networked DDE and OLE 139	
Step by Step 140	

Chapter 9: Network Communications — 147

Dialing In	148
Remote Control 148	
Remote Node 151	
Deciding Factors 157	
Dialing Out	158

Chapter 10: The Workgroup Connection — 163

Installing the Workgroup Connection	164
Using the Workgroup Connection	167
The NET Pop-Up Menu 168	
Loading NET as a TSR Program 169	
Connecting and Disconnecting Network Disks 169	
Connecting and Disconnecting Network Printers 170	
Checking Print Jobs 172	
Using the NET Command-Line Interface	173
The Command-Line Interface 173	
NET.EXE Command-Line Options 174	

Chapter 11: Fine-Tuning Windows for Workgroups — 183

The Windows for Workgroups Initialization Files — 184

Monitoring and Managing Network Activity — 186
- Net Watcher 187
- WinMeter 187
- Controlling Server Performance 189

Managing Print Queues — 190

Defining Additional Printer Ports — 191

Restricting Shared Resources — 191

Inhibiting the Startup Group — 192

Managing Persistent Network Connections — 193

Locking Up the Program Manager — 194

LAN Manager Visibility — 194

Appendix   The Hearts Game: Network Fun! — 197
- Hearts Hints 199

Glossary — 200

Index — 207

■ Acknowledgments

First, to our wives. We couldn't have stayed in the engine room stoking the fires if Becky and Marlene hadn't kept a firm grip on the wheel and maintained things on even keel. Then to Eric Stone, the lookout who suffered constant drenchings, at least from the tears of the self-pitying authors. We must thank Eric Rudder, Steve Rigney, and Geoff LeBlond, who stood superhuman on the rocks and pushed us away when we foundered. And then to the deck crew, the hands who helped make the voyage successful: M. D. Barrera, Howard Blechman, Janna Hecker Clark, Noelle Graney, Cat Haglund, Ami Knox, Melinda Levine, Vanessa Miller, and Valerie Haynes Perry.

■ Introduction

This book is a good investment in the future. We are convinced that Microsoft's Windows for Workgroups will become the most important and the most widely used piece of business software. Windows for Workgroups will change the way people work together and the way they play together. Our goal in writing this book is to help you easily install and effectively use Windows for Workgroups.

In the Windows for Workgroups environment, there isn't a big difference between a user and an administrator. You are largely responsible for sharing and attaching to your own resources. The traditional administrator becomes more of a coordinator and, sometimes, a cheerleader. We've written this book for both the user and the coordinator. We provide everything but the pompoms. We have step-by-step instructions for beginning users, hints and tips for coordinators, and technical discussions concerning installation and configuration options for the technically curious or furious.

Although this book deals with networking, the entire point of the book and of Microsoft's product is that you don't have to be a networking expert to enjoy the benefits of Windows for Workgroups. We explain every buzzword from Ethernet to NetBEUI, describe the standards that apply to wiring and cabling, and introduce you to our tricks, tips, and techniques for networking. But you won't get lost in the process. We provide a complete chapter on network planning, with checklists and guides that help you plan your network up front so you avoid making bad investments while keeping flexibility and room for growth.

Do you need to link your computer into an existing network? We explain how to use Windows for Workgroups on networks with Novell's NetWare, Microsoft's LAN Manager, IBM's LAN Server, Digital's PathWorks, and other network operating systems. We also provide information on how to link Apple Macintosh computers into the Windows for Workgroups system and how to share information between applications on PCs and Macs.

Windows for Workgroups includes an automated installation system that has a high percentage rate of success. But what do you do when things *don't* work? We tell you how to recover when the installation goes wrong and what files you can erase or edit to start over. Throughout the book we have inserted tips on avoiding problems and getting the most from your system. The last chapter in the book contains dozens of potent and distilled tips on using, tuning, and configuring the network.

Windows for Workgroups includes a useful electronic mail package and an application for workgroup scheduling. We give you detailed descriptions of how to use these programs, and we also explain how Microsoft's programs differ from the competition's.

People don't work in just one place anymore. Someone working on the road or at home still needs access to network resources. In this book we provide the information you need and describe the alternatives you can choose to create an economical and efficient remote network access system.

An important innovation in Windows for Workgroups is networked Dynamic Data Exchange (DDE). The name is imposing, but so is the power of this network service. Through networked DDE, you can link the same application or different applications running on different computers so that they automatically update and exchange information. This capability will change the way people prepare reports, handle forms, plan projects, and create ideas. We take you step by step through the menus and windows you use to connect on networked DDE and explain the differences between features such as Paste, Paste Special, linking, and embedding. The path is a little tricky, but we give you a good guide.

No network is really useful without application programs. We explain in general how to install applications and specifically how to install and use Word for Windows, Excel for Windows, 1-2-3 for Windows, Ami Pro, WordPerfect for Windows, and PowerPoint. Some of these programs work better than others on Windows for Workgroups networks, and we discuss why. We also lay out your options for installing programs on local drives and on servers. And we tell you why you might be better off with no floppy-disk drives at all.

Windows for Workgroups is an important product—it's a total network environment that is loaded with features, but you don't have to be a networking expert to use it. We want to help you get the most out of it!

- *The Windows Family*
- *Benefits for NetWare Users*
- *Installation Overview*
- *How Much Horsepower?*
- *Other Servers*
- *Weaving It All Together*
- *The Universal Client*

CHAPTER

1

Networking under Windows for Workgroups

PSYCHOLOGISTS USE THE TERM *AHA! PHENOMENON* TO DESCRIBE what takes place when developments click together and you suddenly see things in a new perspective. Now coming together are developments that should activate the Aha! Phenomenon in you. This book shows you the ins and outs of networking with Microsoft's *Windows for Workgroups*, an enhanced version of Windows with peer-to-peer networking built-in. With this product, any Windows PC can be a server or a client for any other PC running Windows or DOS. But that explanation describes only one development—and it doesn't give you that Aha! feeling yet.

In addition to putting networking in Windows, Microsoft is adding network client software to the MS-DOS version 6.0. Of course many people don't see a need to update their existing versions of Windows or DOS, so Microsoft also offers add-in products that bring networking to existing installations. These products make it easy to add network client services to Windows 3.1 and DOS 5. In this way, any and every PC running DOS can use the attached drives, printers, and communications services of any properly equipped PC running Windows for Workgroups.

In other developments, networking hardware is coming to all PCs. Companies like Artisoft and Eagle Technology are selling small and very inexpensive chip sets for Ethernet. These will encourage manufacturers to add network connections to PCs, modems, printers, and many other devices. IBM has teamed up with National Semiconductor while Texas Instruments and Chips and Technologies are each working separately to bring out chip sets that can operate on either Ethernet or Token-Ring. These chip sets will encourage companies to put networking services into modems, printers, hard-disk drives, and other devices. Networking capabilities will soon be part of all types of computer products.

The prices of LAN adapters, once very high-margin items, have slid so low that it no longer makes sense to market them as options in new computer packages. Instead, a LAN adapter will be a part of the computer—just like the video adapter and hard-disk controller. Already, the entire line of Zenith Data System computers, from notebooks to high-powered servers, has Ethernet networking built-in.

These are the three most important developments:

- Client and server capabilities in Windows
- Client networking services in DOS
- Low-cost network connections on every PC

These developments lead you to a minor Aha! conclusion: ubiquitous networking. But there is more.

In the long run, the most exciting development that Windows for Workgroups brings to the market is its ability to link Windows application programs across networks. Through these networked links, the programs can automatically exchange and modify portions of files and documents. This feature allows you to link specific chunks of spreadsheets, drawings, text files, and other types of data objects into documents and presentations being constructed simultaneously on several networked machines. As one person changes a spreadsheet or drawing, it automatically updates its image wherever it has been pasted into documents and presentations. In the long run, these behind-the-scenes links between programs will change the way end users interact with networks and the way people work together.

If we have ubiquitous and invisible networks with automated links between the applications, a new picture of networking snaps into focus. You shift away from simply sharing your C: drive as the next person's D: drive and fly to doing cooperative and interactive work in real time. You have a completely new way of linking programs that people use for on-line transactions—such jobs as making reservations and taking orders—and a new way to build process modeling and control programs ranging from war games to virus-growth models. You also have an excellent basis for interactive information services or games. Given the nearly automatic installation of the networking software, the work of network managers moves to linking applications, and the work of end users shifts to computer-aided, cooperative workgroup efforts.

■ The Windows Family

It's important to understand how Windows for Workgroups fits in with other Windows products. The Windows family of products has three distinct members: Windows, Windows for Workgroups, and Windows NT, but we believe Windows for Workgroups will become the most important and widely distributed part of the family. Figure 1.1 shows the relationship of the family members.

No matter how much or how little you use Windows, you can't dispute its importance and popularity. In May 1992, Microsoft's monthly shipments of Windows began to surpass those of DOS. Windows comes bundled with—and usually installed on—nine out of ten of the best-selling brands of PCs. Almost all development of PC software is being done under Windows.

Windows for Workgroups expands the power and appeal of Windows by adding connectivity and productivity services. The product gives PCs running Windows the ability to make disk drives, subdirectories, and devices such as CD-ROM drives and attached printers available to other DOS and Windows PCs across a wide variety of network adapters and cabling schemes. PCs running DOS can use the Windows servers by loading the Microsoft Workgroup Connection, a product available separately or through the built-in networking capabilities planned for DOS 6.

Better Than NT?

Windows NT (New Technology) is the third member of the Microsoft Windows family. It includes all the capabilities of Windows for Workgroups, and it layers in other features that corporate system managers, but not necessarily Windows power users, will like.

Chapter 1: Networking under Windows for Workgroups

Figure 1.1

The Windows environment brings multitasking capabilities and the graphical user interface to PCs. A high percentage of Windows is 32-bit code and while it loads over DOS, it largely replaces DOS when it runs. Windows for Workgroups includes the features of Windows and adds the ability to share resources through networking. Windows NT is a bootable operating system; it doesn't need DOS to get started. It adds operating system security and nearly all 32-bit code while retaining all the features of Windows for Workgroups. LAN Manager for NT adds management and network security to NT.

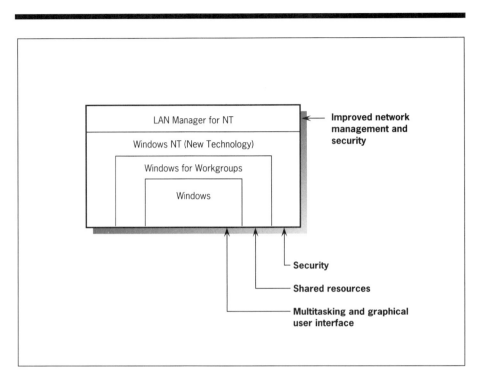

Although Windows NT is widely touted for its 32-bit processing power, its architecture is likely to always make it somewhat slower in basic I/O tasks than Windows for Workgroups. Both Windows and Windows for Workgroups make extensive use of 32-bit operations, but, according to Microsoft, Windows for Workgroups is optimized to make better use of the 32-bit code than is Windows.

Developers can use the WIN32 System Developer's Kit (SDK) to write applications for both Windows for Workgroups and Windows NT. The SDK allows developers to create a single program that will run on both Windows 3.1 and Windows NT. These products can use a 32-bit flat memory model under Windows 3.1 so developers can move data in bigger and more efficient blocks and take advantage of the 32-bit registers in 80386 and 80486 processors.

The strengths and limitations of Windows NT come from the same source: improved security. NT is designed to appeal to government and corporate users by providing data security that meets the U.S. government's C2 rating. But this architecture means that NT must maintain total control and not allow applications to take shortcuts by communicating directly with the hardware. This limitation also restricts the compatibility of any application or driver not written according to specific guidelines.

When combined with Microsoft's LAN Manager for NT, which is designed to provide better security and administration on multiserver networks, Windows NT makes an excellent platform for a high-security corporate file server. Windows NT has the ability to use symmetrical multiprocessing—it can allocate tasks to two or more CPUs simultaneously—on hardware from NCR and other companies, and it will include TCP/IP network drivers. But on the bottom line, if you don't need the high security, added reliability, or symmetrical multiprocessing of Windows NT, choose Windows for Workgroups to run your modern applications and to integrate your networking needs.

Mail and Scheduling

Windows for Workgroups includes a special version of Microsoft Mail 3.0. This product lets you handle the usual electronic mail chores, but it lacks many of the post office management features of the full Microsoft Mail package, and it can't use gateways. Overall, it is an excellent e-mail package for a workgroup of people in a single office, but when you want to add links to other mail systems or to remote callers you'll need either a full version of Microsoft Mail or an optional Microsoft program called the Mail Transfer Agent that completes connections to gateways.

The mail product enables another major application included in the Windows for Workgroups package, Microsoft Schedule+. Microsoft Schedule+ is a full-strength networked scheduling program that allows you to keep your local calendar while also coordinating appointments with others in your workgroup. It reads the list of authorized user names from the mail program and uses mail to communicate throughout the workgroup. The package points out conflicts in the calendars of people you want to invite to meetings, suggests free times, provides reminder alarms, and performs all the other expected functions. In short, it is a full-power scheduling package that competes well with other stand-alone programs.

Unfortunately, because the whole focus of Windows for Workgroups is on computer names instead of on people's names, the mail program can't read user names from a central database as Microsoft Mail can from NetWare. You have to enter each user's name, mailbox name, and an optional password. Keeping this information current can add to the network administrator's chores.

The good news about the mail service is that it will be the underlying "engine" for new workgroup applications that Microsoft and other developers will release starting in early 1993. This is illustrated in Figure 1.2. These products use the concept of business forms to automate and manage interactive work between people in busy offices. The forms pass routing information to the mail system so that some process—for example, accepting a credit application—can be started by one person and routed automatically and simultaneously to other people who work on collateral tasks such as approval and notification. Expect to see more programs for enabling the group process and sharing group memory to emerge as Windows for Workgroups spreads.

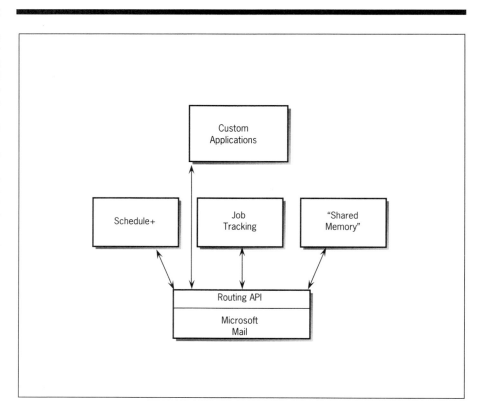

Figure 1.2

The Microsoft Mail system built into Windows for Workgroups will become a "forms engine" designed to automatically route business forms between members of a workgroup. The word *forms* is a broad term encompassing such tasks as scheduling, job tracking, and order taking, gaining access to the combination of message and data called shared memory, and many other specialized applications. These applications address an application program interface (API) in Microsoft Mail to describe the proper routing of the forms. This could be the most effective attempt so far to use a PC application to replace paper.

Networked Dynamic Data Exchange (DDE)

You can use the ability of Windows for Workgroups to link programs today, but more specialized applications with built-in linking will appear in the future. For a present-day example, which is illustrated in Figure 1.3, assume three people have the job of generating a weekly report. One person creates the text and a written document in Microsoft Word, the second person juggles numbers in an Excel spreadsheet, while a third person generates slides in PowerPoint. The person using Word and the person using PowerPoint can paste and link specific segments, selected by the Clipboard Copy command, from the Excel spreadsheet into each application and always have the latest data and interpretation. For example, as the person using PowerPoint moves through the presentation, macros read in the linked elements created by the other programs. The other programs don't have to be active, but the files must be linked either automatically through macros or manually through the shared ClipBook.

Figure 1.3

A person working on the PC labeled Source creates a bar chart in a spreadsheet. Using menu commands contained in Windows for Workgroups, this chart is available for linking across the LAN. The people using word processing and presentation software at the other PCs link to the shared chart and integrate it into documents and presentations. There are various linking options, but in the most complex link-up, all people see the changes simultaneously as any one person changes the chart.

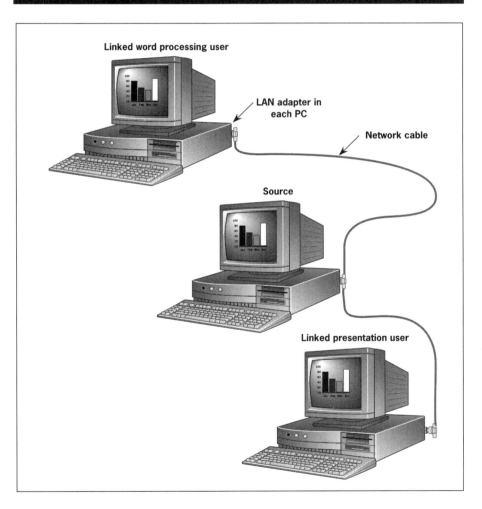

Linking applications through macros is a task for someone with programming skills, but anyone can establish links through the menus. If you've practiced the steps, which aren't completely intuitive, using the ClipBook is simple. Once one person copies an object—a piece of a picture, text, or spreadsheet—into a shared ClipBook, it can appear on all other Windows for Workgroups PCs as a selection in the ClipBook viewer, a new utility in the Windows Main group. The shared ClipBook can be password protected if you want to restrict access. We illustrate the Copy-share-Paste process in Chapter 8, but the choices and options can be confusing if you don't practice the skills often.

Although a few network managers will tackle writing the macros needed to integrate a weekly report, developers will provide many specialized applications. This architecture can challenge present-day database technology in many transaction-processing applications. It provides an excellent way to track projects and to manage work, and it's a great basis for building interactive games.

■ Benefits for NetWare Users

Microsoft made a smart move by bundling into Windows for Workgroups the client software for Novell's NetWare. The NetWare client software and a special version of Netware's IPX are options you can load during installation or at a later time. Under Windows for Workgroups, you can simultaneously log in to other Windows PCs and to NetWare servers. The NetWare server can even host the Microsoft Mail network mailbox—actually a file subdirectory on the server.

In effect, present users of NetWare can add the functions of Windows for Workgroups and never lose the dedicated NetWare features. You can have the shared links between applications offered by Windows for Workgroups and the elaborate server management, communications, and routing features of the higher-powered NetWare server software at the same time. Some users on the network can elect to make disk drives, shared printers, or CD-ROM drives available through Windows while everyone still uses the dedicated server for primary file operations.

If you don't want to contribute or use shared drives under Windows for Workgroups, you don't have to. But if you want to take advantage of available resources it's easy to do so: They simply appear as more DOS disk-drive letters or LPT ports. You can use the drag-and-drop file transfer feature of the Windows File Manager on all networked and local drives.

■ Installation Overview

Microsoft's goal of providing invisible and ubiquitous networking requires nearly automatic installation. Windows for Workgroups has the unique ability to recognize and automatically load drivers for nearly 200 different makes and models of LAN adapters. If the adapter can be totally configured by software, as many products from Intel, 3Com, Madge, SMC, and other vendors can be, then the software takes care of everything. If the adapter has jumpers or switches, the software asks you to confirm the default settings or to enter new settings. You'll get truly automatic and seamless network installations only in PCs with fully programmable or on-the-motherboard LAN adapters, but the software will give you hints about interrupt request (IRQ) and memory address combinations even for hardware-selectable adapters.

During the installation process, which is described in detail in Chapter 3, you can elect to load NetWare client software and drivers in addition to the Windows for Workgroups protocols. The NetWare drivers are standard Novell code, and all of the memory-management tricks and tribulations of loading NetWare under Windows apply. Of course you can't load the NetWare drivers into extended memory because that is used by Windows. However, having the drivers in the Windows package and automatically installed is a big plus.

One aspect of Windows for Workgroups that will irritate anyone using a version of DOS before 6.0 is its insistence on loading network drivers in the CONFIG.SYS file through DEVICE= statements. If you should not want to run Windows, or if you want to exit Windows to work under DOS, you'll lose (depending on the adapter) 10–16K of memory to unused drivers. The installation program makes changes to your CONFIG.SYS, AUTOEXEC.BAT, and WIN.INI files without asking or telling you about the changes.

Automatic installation also means single-minded installation. If everything goes right the first time, installations are a snap. But sometimes when we made a mistake, particularly in naming people and mailboxes in the MS Mail program, it was difficult to backtrack. Often it was easier to edit an .INI file with a DOS text editor or even to erase an entire .INI file to force the program to start over than to change a configuration through the program.

Through the File Manager and Print Manager programs in Windows, you set up the initial profile of the drives and printers that you want to make available to the network and of the network resources you want to use. The program icons are the same as those in Windows, but the Toolbar in each program has special share and connect icons, and the pull-down menus include those functions, as well. Once you make the selection, it is written into WIN.INI.

If anything, Microsoft might have made it a little too easy to stop sharing a subdirectory, drive, or printer. There are warnings if other PCs are attached to a shared drive, but with a few mouse clicks, you can cause someone to lose the ability to save a file.

If you elect to load NetWare, you use the standard NetWare Map utility to select those resources. Of course, you have to avoid disk-drive letters already used or potentially used by Windows for Workgroups for shared drives.

Chapter 3 presents a complete explanation of Windows for Workgroups installation.

■ How Much Horsepower?

The question of how much processing power it takes to be a Windows for Workgroups server has one answer: It depends. The only requirement to act as a server is that Windows for Workgroups must run in enhanced mode.

If a person is a heavy user of Windows applications, keeps multiple applications open, generates a large number of system interrupts by using many keystrokes, and if the network users will write to the shared hard drive often, then the fastest available processor and about 16 megabytes of RAM are in order. But if the PC sits idle most of the time and the network is lightly used, then even a 386SX/25 with 4 megabytes of memory will work well enough for most installations.

During our hands-on testing, the effect of RAM on processing speed under Windows became very clear. PCs with 16 or even 8 megabytes of memory snapped screens into place while otherwise identical machines with 4 megabytes of memory took much longer to create the screens. A 386DX/33 with 8 megabytes of RAM and a 200+ megabyte IDE hard drive is the combination we'd recommend for a reasonable Windows for Workgroups server.

■ Other Servers

Windows for Workgroups uses the proven Microsoft SMB (Server Message Block) client/server protocol, shown in Figure 1.4, on top of the NetBEUI network communications protocols—an extension, developed by Microsoft and IBM, of the NetBIOS (Network Basic Input/Output System) protocols. As an SMB/NetBEUI client and server, PCs running Windows for Workgroups can interact with other programs in the same family, such as Microsoft LAN Manager, IBM LAN Server, and Digital's Pathworks. The NDIS (Network Driver Interface Specification) layer software makes it possible to replace or augment NetBEUI with other drivers such as NetWare's IPX or TCP/IP.

Other companies, notably Artisoft and Sitka, have done an excellent job of integrating peer-to-peer networking into Windows. Both Artisoft's LANtastic for Windows and Sitka's 10NET for Windows take excellent advantage of the graphical user interface and LANtastic extends the power of Dynamic Data Exchange (DDE) across the network. We particularly like the drag-and-drop resource selection feature of LANtastic for Windows.

Figure 1.4

In the Windows for Workgroups default networking scheme, when an application program on the client PC makes a request to DOS, the request is redirected to the Server Message Block (SMB) software for formatting. The SMB request moves to the NetBEUI software for encapsulation and then through the NDIS layer and on to the LAN adapter for transmission across the network. At the server, the packet is received by a LAN adapter, the data envelope is stripped off by NetBEUI, and the request is routed to the SMB. The SMB passes the request through the file and print services module for security and then to the file system for action.

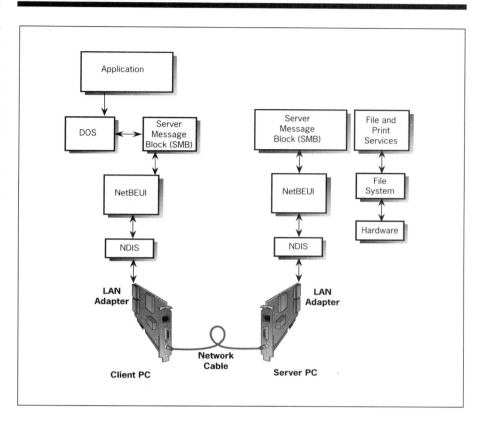

However, both LANtastic for Windows and 10NET are add-ins. You can hopelessly confuse the selection of networked drives and shared resources in either product by logging in to different server drives in separate virtual Windows sessions—something that the tight integration of Windows for Workgroups, with its networking software, doesn't allow. Neither company can hope to have its product be as widely packaged or distributed as Windows for Workgroups.

The only hole in Microsoft's strategy, one that companies like Performance Technology, Sitka, and 10NET Communications Systems (which has a complex marketing agreement with Sitka) can exploit, is the lack of a DOS-based server alternative in Windows for Workgroups. The similar SMB NetBIOS architectures of POWERLan and 10NET mark them as excellent DOS-based servers for Windows for Workgroups clients. You can load a POWERLan server, noted for fast performance under DOS, or a 10NET server and share its resources with Windows for Workgroups clients with no changes on the Windows PCs.

However, interaction with such products as Pathworks, POWERLan, or 10NET isn't automatic. Because there is no firm specification for the network function called browsing, the 10NET and POWERLan servers probably will not show up as choices in the Windows resource selection boxes; the servers have no standard way to advertise their services across the network. But if you manually enter the server name and shared resource name, the service will connect. After the first connection, Windows for Workgroups will remember how to make the link.

The interaction between Windows for Workgroup and IBM's LAN Server is limited by the different security concepts of the products, so you'll have to use \\server\share names instead of the aliases that make LAN Server easier to manage.

You can use the Windows for Workgroups client software with a Microsoft LAN Manager server running over OS/2, and you can use the Macintosh interface in LAN Manager to link to Macintosh computers and bring the Mac files and services to the Windows PCs. Microsoft's Mail and Schedule products for the Macintosh interoperate with those in Windows for Workgroups. Chapter 7 details OS/2 and Macintosh links to Windows for Workgroups under LAN Manager.

■ Weaving It All Together

Figure 1.5 shows a practical network configuration with three networked PCs, a Macintosh, and three dedicated servers. It illustrates the wide number of resources available to a Windows for Workgroups client PC. You might have a lot more PCs on your network, but each additional PC would probably be configured like one of the three in this example.

In Figure 1.5, the PC on the left, labeled Power User PC, is a Windows for Workgroups server, so people working at the other two client PCs can access its hard-disk drive and send print jobs to its attached printer. This machine is also a Windows for Workgroups client, so it can access other Windows for Workgroups servers and the dedicated servers running LAN Manager and POWERLan or 10NET without any additional software. In our example, the person using this PC also wants to access the NetWare server simultaneously, so the Novell IPX and shell are also loaded.

NOTE. *Because of the processing and memory requirements, you won't have many machines running as much software as the Power User PC is in Figure 1.5. This machine should probably be at least a 386DX/33 with 8 megabytes of RAM.*

Figure 1.5

PCs running Windows for Workgroups can act as clients for servers running a variety of network operating systems.

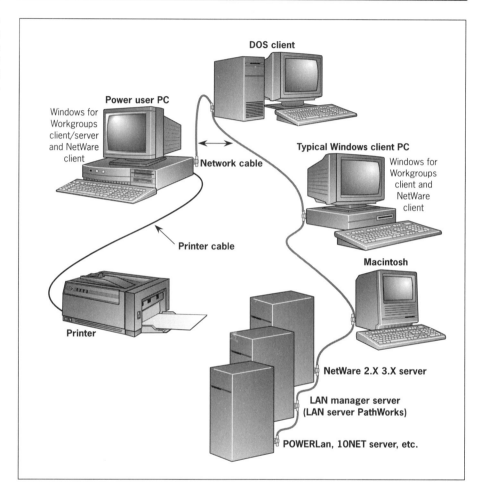

The PC labeled the Typical Windows Client is a client to any server running Windows for Workgroups, LAN Manager, or other SMB/NetBIOS software such as POWERLan or 10NET. Even though this PC is not configured as a Windows server, the person using it has the full ability to make data objects available to other Windows for Workgroups PCs through the network ClipBook. This PC also has NetWare client software loaded, so it can use any available NetWare file, printing, and communications services.

The PC labeled DOS client is running the Microsoft Workgroup Connection, SMB/NetBIOS client software for DOS. This PC is a client to the

Windows for Workgroups servers and the LAN Manager and PowerLan or 10NET servers. This PC has no access to the network ClipBook.

The Macintosh can share files with the PCs through software running on the NetWare or LAN Manager servers.

The Novell, LAN Manager, POWERLan, and 10NET servers are optional. The LAN Manager server could also be a Digital Pathworks server running over VMS or Unix or it could be an IBM LAN Server running over OS/2. You can configure the POWERLan and 10NET products as client/server PCs or as dedicated servers.

■ The Universal Client

It is interesting to apply the lesson of Macintosh networking to Windows for Workgroups. Apple built good networking software into the Mac, but made it difficult for other companies to add their networking software into the computer. Companies such as Novell, Microsoft, and Banyan had to make major adaptations to accept the native Mac as a client under their server software.

It is easy to predict the same future for Windows for Workgroups. It has its own tightly integrated networking system, while software for other network products is clearly an add-in. Because of the complexity of the Windows environment, many networking companies will find it easier to make servers for Windows client PCs than to add their own software into Windows. People in the industry have discussed adding SMB over NetBIOS services to NetWare for years. We predict that it won't be long before Windows for Workgroups PCs are the universal clients able to simultaneously use the services of any major server and peer PCs without loading extra software. Aha! Get the picture?

- *Taking an Inventory*
- *Defining Your Requirements*
- *Core Planning Issues*
- *Additional Planning Factors*

CHAPTER 2

Planning Your Network

THE RULE OF THE FOUR Ps—PLANNING PRECLUDES POOR PERFORmance—should govern the early phase of every network installation. A little up-front work can save weeks of corrections and additions. In many cases, we mean literally a "little" planning; sometimes ten minutes of investigation is all you need. But any network with a dozen or more PCs will require you to spend a couple of hours and prepare a couple of pages of information before you place your first order for equipment and wiring. Even though Windows for Workgroups has tightly integrated networking capabilities and can often successfully install itself, there is still much planning you must do to create a successful network.

This chapter is designed to help anyone with an existing network or anyone planning a network to identify the important network planning factors. The planning process has two major physical components: the inventory and the statement of requirements. With these two packages of information in hand, you can plan the kind of server, wiring, memory, and client PC configurations you need.

■ Taking an Inventory

Before you start any network installation, you need a detailed inventory of the PCs and printers that will be in the network. Figure 2.1 is an inventory sheet that you should prepare for every networked PC.

Note that the inventory sheet asks for a great deal of information on the devices inside of and attached to each PC. Since each PC in a Windows for Workgroups network is capable of sharing all its resources with other PCs across the network, you need a detailed view of the available devices. Every piece of information is potentially valuable.

For example, you might not think the type of video adapter in a PC has anything to do with its networking capabilities, but information about the video adapter is important for two reasons.

First, during installation you decide whether to use memory-management software that loads network drivers above the portion of each PC's memory used by typical DOS applications. Some video adapters take up a great deal of the potentially free memory above 640K, leaving little room for pieces of the network operating system in that high memory. To make an informed decision about memory-management software, you need to know what kind of adapter each PC has.

Second, it is often useful to be able to remotely control a PC across a LAN using a product such as Artisoft's Network Eye, or across a telephone line using a modem remote-control program such as Norton-Lambert's Close-Up or Co/Session from Triton Technologies. These programs, which let you see and control what is happening on the client computer, are useful for training people on applications, troubleshooting, and configuring workstations. However, you often can't control a PC that has one type of video from a PC that has a different type, so it's important to know what kind of video board is in every PC.

Figure 2.1

This detailed questionnaire helps you gather the information you need to plan the sharing of the network's printers, hard drives, and other resources. Information on the number of slots, memory address, and interrupt request (IRQ) lines available and in use is important when you're planning what adapters to buy and how to configure the networking software.

Network Survey Form   Date:
Name of this machine's primary user:
Extension number and department:
Brand name on the PC:
Brand name and model on the monitor:
If a printer is attached, brand name and model:
Is the printer connected via serial or parallel?
If a modem is attached, brand name and model:
    Speed:
    Internal or external?
CD-ROM SCSI memory address:
What is the primary application used at the PC?
How many serial ports in this machine?
    COM1: 9 or 25 pin?
    COM2: 9 or 25 pin?
What is attached to the serial ports?
    COM1:
    COM2:
How many parallel ports?
How many free expansion slots?
Type of CPU: Speed:
Type of BIOS: Date:
Separate mouse board?
What size floppy-disk drives?
    5$\frac{1}{4}$ Density?
    3$\frac{1}{2}$ Density?
What size hard-disk drive?
Amount of free disk space:
How much total memory reported?
What is reported in memory? (Device drivers and TSRs?)
Other devices:
How could this PC be attached to a network cable?
    Unshielded twisted-pair available?
    Could we run coax to this location?

HINT. *You should keep your inventory on a PC-by-PC basis, categorized by department, but you'll also find valuable a cross index by PC type. A simple database program will let you sort on any factor and generate reports. We find that printed reports kept in a three-ring binder provide fast reference. Remember, you might not be able to access the server holding the database you need if the network is down!*

A number of programs can provide you with the information you need to complete the inventory sheet. Microsoft includes a program in the Windows package called MSD.EXE (Microsoft Diagnostics) that can produce detailed reports showing how a PC is configured. System Sleuth from Dariana Technology Group is also an excellent aid for anyone who has to install a LAN adapter in an already crowded PC. Both programs survey the PC and provide information on all aspects of the system from the disk drives to the memory map. The programs scan for active and inactive IRQ (interrupt request line) locations and help you determine where you can squeeze in a LAN card or other expansion device.

Finding the inventory sheets when you need them is just as important as completing them in the first place. Keep the sheets someplace where you can always find them, and be sure to update them for every change. Although we suggest using a three-ring binder to hold all the inventory sheets, we've also seen successful installations in which each PC's inventory sheet was kept in an envelope taped to its side.

■ Defining Your Requirements

What do you and the other people who will use the network want it to do? Figure 2.2 provides a set of questions you can use to define your expectations and requirements. You might have to research questions such as those concerning the amount of RAM required by terminate-and-stay-resident programs (TSRs), but such information is necessary. Despite the widespread use of memory-management software, RAM cram is still a major problem in PCs running DOS, and you need to keep a close watch on the amount of free RAM below 640K in each machine that doesn't run Windows full time.

HINT. *Users often don't know what they want from a network before it's installed and will sometimes suffer in silence once it's in because they think their problem is silly or their own fault. Talk frequently to the people using the network; many of their minor problems will be easy to solve.*

Figure 2.2

The answers to these questions will help you project needs for hard-disk space, remote-access connections, cabling, and other requirements.

We want to help you get the most value from your computer system. Please answer these few questions so we can give you enough resources to meet your needs.

Name:

Department and telephone extension:

How many sheets of paper do you print in an average week? If the number varies widely from week to week, please give a range:

Please list the programs you use. If you aren't sure of a program's name, enter its function:

Do you have to exchange files on a floppy disk or by some other means with anyone?   If so, how often and who is the other person(s)?

Are there files you need to see or use on any other PC within the organization? Please explain:

Do you ever have to move to someone else's PC to do a job? If so, what job, and why do you have to move?

Are there some jobs you would like to be able to do on your computer, but can't? Please explain:

Do you know of any plans to change the location of your desk or computer in the near future?

■ Core Planning Issues

Once you know what you have on hand and what you want to accomplish, you can begin looking at some specific planning issues. Three vital factors require up-front decisions that you'll probably have to live with for a long time:

- Physical configuration (adapters and cabling)
- Server(s)
- Printers

Crossing Adapters and Cabling

Choosing the right network media access control architecture (the way adapters share the network cable) and network cabling scheme is important, but often you can make your decision by answering a few quick questions. The information in this book will help you make those decisions, but if you want to know more about the nitty-gritty of LAN media access control protocols and cabling, we suggest you read the second edition of *PC Magazine Guide to Connectivity,* written by Frank Derfler and published by Ziff-Davis Press.

The choices between a network media access control scheme and the type of cable you use are independent of each other. LAN adapters on the market for the three leading access schemes, ARCnet, Ethernet, and Token-Ring, can use a variety of cables.

Windows for Workgroups does not do a good job of supporting LAN adapters using the ARCnet standard. Although ARCnet still works well in many installations, it has been eclipsed by the 10BaseT form of Ethernet, which uses unshielded twisted-pair wire. So in a Windows for Workgroups LAN, your two choices are some form of Ethernet or Token-Ring LAN adapters.

The choice comes down to cost and the need for mainframe access. Token-Ring offers very high reliability and the ability to connect directly into IBM mainframe and midrange computers. Typically, if you are going to need Token-Ring, you will know it early because you'll be influenced by the need for IBM connectivity. The downside of Token-Ring is its price. Token-Ring adapters typically cost twice as much as those designed for Ethernet.

Ethernet systems are extremely popular. New installations typically use unshielded twisted-pair wire, the 10BaseT standard, to link each PC to a central wiring hub. If your network has only a few nodes, however, we suggest using a slightly different Ethernet wiring scheme known as *thin net*—coaxial cable that runs from PC to PC and uses T-connectors to make the connection at each PC. Microsoft is marketing an installation kit that includes two copies of Windows for Workgroups, two Intel adapters, and the coaxial cable and connectors you need to link two PCs.

The major drawback to thin net is the fact that if one connection is bad, the entire network fails. If you have more than a handful of PCs, we recommend using the 10BaseT wiring scheme. This scheme adds approximately $80 per PC to the price of an installation due to the cost of a wiring hub, but the improved reliability is worth the up-front cost. Note that several adapters on the market, such as Artisoft's AE-3, can work either with unshielded twisted-pair wire in a 10BaseT star wiring arrangement or with thin Ethernet cable in a station-to-station wiring scheme. If you use an adapter like this, you have room for change in the future.

If you have existing LAN adapters and cabling, you should estimate the cost of staying with that system. If not, your primary concern will be whether your building has existing unshielded twisted-pair wiring that conforms to the 10BaseT specifications for Ethernet or to the IBM Type 3 cable specifications for Token-Ring—and if so, whether it terminates in a central wiring closet.

You must look carefully at the quality of the cable used in any installation, old or new. It seems that every international and national organization even remotely concerned with networking has issued standards or guidelines for LAN cabling. The National Electrical Code describes various types of cables and the materials used in them, and IBM has its own family of cable specifications. In addition, the Electronic Industries Association/Telecommunications Industry Association (EIA/TIA) has issued EIA/TIA 568 and 569 standards for technical performance and has an active program to extend its requirements. The Institute of Electrical and Electronic Engineers (IEEE) also includes minimal cable requirements in its 802.3 and 802.5 specifications for Ethernet and Token-Ring systems.

HINT. *The star wiring configuration used in 10BaseT systems is generally more reliable than the thin Ethernet cable installed in a station-by-station wiring scheme, simply because the station-to-station cable has so many potential points of failure. We strongly recommend you choose a star wiring configuration of coaxial or unshielded twisted-pair wiring for bet-the-business network applications.*

The Underwriters Laboratory (UL) focuses on safety standards, but it has expanded its certification program to evaluate twisted-pair LAN cables for performance according to IBM and EIA/TIA performance specifications as well as National Electrical Code safety specifications. The program UL has established to mark shielded and unshielded twisted-pair LAN cables should simplify the complex task of making sure the materials used in the installation are up to specification.

The UL markings range from Level I through Level V. IBM's cable specifications range from Type 1 through Type 9; the EIA/TIA has proposed categories of 1 through 5. It's easy to become confused by the similarly numbered levels, types, and categories. The IBM type specifications include descriptions of the configuration of each cable type, such as two pairs of 22-AWG shielded nonplenum cable. The UL level markings deal with performance and safety, but don't specify the details such as shielded or unshielded wire included in the IBM specifications. Like the UL levels, the emerging EIA/TIA categories will focus on performance.

Note that simply using the right materials doesn't guarantee that an installation meets performance specifications. Many factors, including how much the wire is untwisted before it reaches a terminal block, the type of terminal block, the electrical noise in various frequency bands, and the near-end crosstalk (NEXT) caused by wires in proximity to each other determine the quality of the total installation. You can obtain a good reliable start on an installation by using the correct cable, however.

Cables certified with UL Level I and II markings meet safety requirements, but the lower-level markings don't tell you much about performance. The primary difference between cables with Levels III, IV, and V UL markings is in the maximum amount of attenuation and crosstalk allowed in different frequency bands. Cables with higher UL number markings have lower attenuation and crosstalk; they will typically allow higher practical signaling speeds through the wiring system. The crosstalk and attenuation have to get pretty bad before they slow the network noticeably, but these factors are the major cause of annoying network problems that seem to come and go mysteriously.

The UL-certification marking level isn't all you need to know about a cable—you must provide other specifics to define its exact configuration. The UL certification program also begs the question, "What is the minimum UL-certification marking level I need for the cables in my installation?" The answer is that UL Level III is probably good enough for all of today's installations, but if you someday plan to run 100 megabits per second over your copper cable system, price cables with higher certification levels to see if improved performance in the future is worth an investment today.

Our advice about fiber-optic cabling is clear and conservative. First, if you have a large installation or a noisy electrical environment such as a manufacturing plant, always use fiber between wiring closets in the building and around the campus regardless of what cabling you run between the wiring closets and the desktops.

Second, if you are planning a new building or doing a major rewiring and decide to install unshielded twisted-pair wire, pull as much fiber with it as you can afford and let the fiber sit dark and unused in the walls until the price of the adapters comes into reach. If you install coaxial cable or shielded twisted-pair wiring to each desktop, it isn't necessary to back it up with fiber.

In any case, we recommend using a wiring contractor or electrician who specializes in networking as at least a consultant for the work. Many large organizations have in-house staff who know where the conduits and access points are, but to do the job properly, you need some expertise.

Server Requirements

You must make several decisions about the PCs that will act as servers in your network: What type of CPU to use in each server, how much memory to install, whether to use the server for other tasks, and how much hard-disk storage space to provide.

One primary advantage of Windows for Workgroups over other network operating systems is its ability to make any networked PC running Windows in enhanced mode act as a server while still running application programs. Under Windows for Workgroups, any PC can make its hard-disk drives, printers, modems, CD-ROM drives, and other devices available to PCs across the network. In an extreme case, any single client PC can use dozens of servers. The hard-disk drives of servers appear as different DOS disk-drive letters to each client. Note, however, that handling requests for service from client PCs as a background task takes up space on a server's hard-disk drive and slows the foreground processing of application programs.

You can create a network in which one or many PCs act as servers and run application programs simultaneously, or you can dedicate one or more PCs to the server role. Acting as a server creates a lot of overhead, so be sure any machine working simultaneously in both roles has enough processing power and storage space for both tasks.

It's impossible to specify what computer would be sufficiently powerful and the most economical as a server in every installation. The amount of work done at each client PC, the amount of data stored on the file server, and the load that any particular application places on the server all vary widely. Nonetheless, we'll try to give you some rough rules of thumb.

Not all servers are file servers. Under Windows for Workgroups you can set up some PCs as only print servers or communications servers. File-server actions create the most overhead on a PC because they occupy the PC's processor for many milliseconds at a time. A very busy print server will also bog down if it is feeding a slow printer, but the large amount of memory available in modern printers usually speeds the throughput of print jobs.

If you're creating a file server that will be used by more than 2 or 3 client PCs and will run a low-demand application such as a lightly used word processor at the same time, that server will need a processor in at least the 80386SX 25MHz class. If you want to support 4 to 12 client PCs with file service from the same machine, its processor will have to be in at least the 80386DX 33MHz class. If the PC is going to run a more demanding application, you will either need to moderate the loads of the client stations or provide a powerful processor in the 80486 33MHz, or better, class. We also recommend using a top-end machine for a file server if you plan to support a dozen or more clients.

HINT. *Don't scrimp on the hard-disk drives for a PC that will act as a file server. Buy the biggest and fastest drive(s) you can afford. You'll always find uses for the storage space, and a fast drive is more important to network performance than is a fast processor.*

Some applications that you might not immediately classify as demanding can slow the network operation on a shared-use file server simply because they involve many keystrokes. Keystrokes create hardware interrupts that can delay network processing, so even if the application on the shared server is a simple word processing program, try to assign that machine to someone who doesn't pound the keyboard all day.

Any PC acting as a server will benefit from having several megabytes of memory for a disk cache. Considering the low cost of RAM, it makes sense to have a minimum of 8 megabytes of memory in a Windows for Workgroups file server.

You should also consider two other issues when you plan your servers: power and security. Every PC acting as a server should be protected by an uninterruptable power supply (UPS). People are often confused by the ratings of UPS systems and PC power supplies. UPS systems are typically rated in volt/amps (VA) and PCs are rated in watts. You can usually find a PC's power consumption (in watts) on a plate or sticker on the back of the machine. As a quick rule of thumb, you should choose your UPS with a VA rating of at least twice the wattage rating of the PC power supply it is to support. UPS systems rated at 600 VA are commonly available, and that is about the lowest rating you should accept for the UPS protecting a server.

HINT. *Don't forget to provide a small UPS for the wiring center if you use a star wiring system outside the server. A 10BaseT network will fail completely if the wiring center loses power.*

It's common to overlook physical security for important network file servers. Most managers limit access to important data across the network with a password protection scheme, but many forget that anyone who can touch the server's keyboard can access all the files on its hard drives. If you have sensitive financial or personnel data, consider providing the same level of physical security for the file server PC that you would for the documents it contains. Putting the unit in a private office is usually sufficient, but in some cases you might have to put it in a closet or room that locks. If you do, remember to allow for environmental control of that space to prevent overheating.

Those Darn Printers

Printers are valuable, necessary, and troublesome. Because they are electro-mechanical devices, they break. Since they are often physically distant from the people who use them and can't send messages like "paper out" back through the network, networked printers can create unique administrative problems.

Programs create print jobs in many formats. Sometimes they send the job in a configuration meant for a specific make and model of printer. Sophisticated programs may generate printed output in a page description language such as Adobe's PostScript or Hewlett-Packard's PCL. To avoid problems, you must carefully link the application to the printer through the redirected LPT or COM port in the client PC. The combination of various printers and applications can create a complex matrix for any network planner.

HINT. *Load your laser printers with the maximum amount of memory they will hold. Printers with more memory unload print jobs from the print server faster, so printer memory is a good investment in performance.*

Along with pairing programs and printers, you must also consider the physical location of the printers. People don't want to walk too far to pick up a print job, and jobs that lay in a printer's output tray too long can get lost. Fortunately, Windows for Workgroups lets you attach a printer to any networked PC, so you have some flexibility in physical placement.

Our experience shows that people like to hear the printer start their print jobs. The sound seems to give users a sense of accomplishment (Done at last!). Try to place shared printers at a convenient distance from the people who use them.

■ Additional Planning Factors

You'll live with the physical configuration of the network, the server, and the printers you set up for a long time, but other up-front choices are relatively easy to change:

- Server directory structure
- Network security
- Menus for DOS PCs
- Backup
- Training

The Server Directory Structure

Where you put your subdirectories does make a difference. A sound decision about the logical structure of your server's hard-disk drives makes training and backup easier and simplifies the management of the server.

First, don't put everything into the root directory of the server. Watch the installation programs contained in the applications you install, and override them if they don't start from a subdirectory you designate.

For backup and security purposes, it is often useful to store files created by applications under a major subdirectory name that describes the person or department using those applications. Therefore, all the data files for the spreadsheet, word processing, and accounting programs used in the accounting department could be stored in subdirectories under the major heading "accounts." You can either put the files containing the programs themselves in subdirectories under the same major subdirectory or group them logically by function. If you want to reduce the load on the network, run as many applications as possible from each PC's local C drive.

HINT. *Many DOS word processing programs have large overlay files, sometimes in excess of 600K, which they refer to while performing special tasks such as spelling checks. Loading at least these overlay files on the local drives of networked PCs reduces the load on the server and improves performance. You might have to check with the company that wrote the software to determine the best configuration for the program's files on a network.*

Menu Systems

Menu systems:

- 👍 Make applications easier to use
- 👍 Simplify training
- 👍 Enhance security
- 👍 Help protect against viruses
- 👎 Often require customization

The issues of ease of use, security, and protection against viruses are all legs of the same elephant. Fortunately, several companies market excellent menu programs that provide tools for handling these problems on PCs running DOS.

There's a famous computer-industry adage: "Easy to use is easy to say!" Many people using PCs on a network don't want to know much about computers. The best thing you can do for them is to arrange their systems to start up in the application they'll be using. The catch is, most people use more than one application, so the next best thing you can do is provide a menu that starts applications with a single keystroke.

In its simplest form, a menu program for DOS applications contains a series of commands or batch files that change the command line to the proper drive and subdirectory, start applications, and return the user to a selection screen when applications terminate. More complex menuing programs check for viruses in the programs they run and prevent users from circumventing the menu system.

PC Tools from Central Point Software, Inc.; Direct Net from Fifth Generation Systems, Inc.; and Norton Commander from Symantec are all excellent multipurpose programs that include strong menu systems. Using these tools, you can create a menu system customized to each individual or workgroup. You can even deny access to the DOS command line to prevent copying and protect the system from computer viruses.

Network Security

Network security is an ongoing task that faces every administrator. New people come in, others leave, and some change jobs within the organization. Each action requires a reaction from the network administrator. If you organize the subdirectories and files on your network in a logical and disciplined order, you can easily give people use of the files they need and change their access when they change their jobs.

But there is more to network security than assigning passwords to users and granting access to specific files; viruses are an important subcategory of the security issue. Although a few companies have unknowingly shipped commercial programs containing viruses, they typically enter organizations and networks through illegally copied and pirated software. Your first defense against viruses is a ban against loading any software that you haven't provided and checked yourself. Removing the DOS icon from Program Manager or installing a menu program on DOS PCs that prevents unlimited access to DOS can help to enforce such a ban. You can set up icons and menu selections that perform needed DOS functions such as formatting a floppy or copying a predefined set of files to or from a floppy, but you can also protect the entire network from harm with a menu system.

In addition, we suggest you run a high-quality and frequently updated virus-scanning program from the AUTOEXEC.BAT file of every PC in your organization.

Backup

A good backup system can save your job. Hard-disk subsystems break and people make mistakes, so you can lose data. Early in the network planning cycle, you should decide whether you need special equipment to back up your data files. When you choose a backup storage system, you measure storage capacity and speed against cost. The choices range from floppy-disk drives to 2-gigabyte DAT tape systems. In the middle ground, many people are happy with a quarter-inch tape cartridge (QIC) system that has 120 megabytes of storage (typically called a QIC-120 system). We've also had good results with removable-cartridge disks such as the SyQuest SyDOS and Iomega Bernoulli units.

We suggest you make a regular, periodic backup—perhaps weekly—of all application program files and data files on the file server. Then you can make faster daily backups of only changed data files. This technique saves a lot of time, overall. If you have to restore the server's drive, you first use the full set of files and then the latest set of changed files.

HINT. *You can use the network to back up all the files in all the client PCs, too. During a period of low activity, run a batch file to load the 10NET or PowerLan server software in each DOS machine. Then one machine equipped with a storage device can—again, under the control of batch files you've created—draw down the changed files from each PC.*

Training

We strongly suggest that you plan a short but formal training program for people who will use the network. If you have asked for requirements, planned carefully, set up menus and batch files, and automated the backup process, the training should be painless, but it's still necessary. To make people feel comfortable and confident, you must introduce them to their new set of shared resources.

- *Hardware Installation*
- *Windows for Workgroups Installation*

CHAPTER

3

Installing Windows for Workgroups

ALTHOUGH WINDOWS FOR WORKGROUPS IS USUALLY EASY TO install and configure, today's complicated PC systems can open up a world of possible conflicts and incompatibilities. In this chapter, we'll take a close look at the installation of the Windows software, as well as some typical network hardware.

Before you install Windows for Workgroups, you'll need to take stock of what you already have. You may have an existing network running under an operating system like NetWare or LAN Manager, and you may already have network hardware and software installed in your PC. In most cases, the Windows setup program will automatically recognize your existing network and will install Windows for Workgroups to operate in conjunction with your existing network. The setup program does a commendable job of spotting existing network hardware, but you'll still need to know what specific type of network adapter board and networking software you have installed.

If you're installing Windows for Workgroups as a new, stand-alone network, you'll need to install your network interface boards before you run the Windows setup program. Proper hardware installation can be tricky, especially in PCs with many expansion options. We'll begin by taking a close look at some typical hardware installation problems.

■ Hardware Installation

In order to connect to a network, all network PCs need some type of physical connection to each other. This is most often accomplished by a network interface card, or NIC, connected to a network cable. A NIC is a printed circuit board that is installed in one of the PC's expansion slots. The board connects to the PC's internal data bus, and a connector on the board attaches to the network cable.

For the most part, network boards can be installed only in desktop PCs; most laptops and notebooks don't have the expansion space required by a network board. Those portables can still connect to the network, however, through an external LAN adapter attached to the computer's parallel printer port.

Finding a Home for Your NIC board

If your PC is fairly basic, installing a network interface board is usually a simple matter. In most cases, you can just remove the cover from the PC, find an empty expansion slot, and plug the board into the slot. You don't need to concern yourself with the nitty-gritty details of hardware installation if your PC is fairly basic.

If your PC is already full of expansion boards, you may find that installing a network board causes conflicts with other boards in your system. PCs have a limited number of expansion interface slots, memory addresses, IRQ (interrupt request) lines, and DMA (Direct Memory Access) channels. Video adapters, disk controllers, mouse ports, and communications boards all consume these resources in their host PCs. Table 3.1 shows some of the I/O addresses and IRQ lines used by standard PC devices.

Table 3.1

These IRQ addresses and memory locations commonly interfere with the operation of LAN adapters. Try the LAN adapter with the default settings first. If they don't work, then look for other unused combinations.

IRQ LINE	DEVICE
2	Interrupt controller (use with care in AT-type systems)
3	Serial ports COM2 and COM4, many network boards
4	Serial ports COM1 and COM3
5	Second parallel port, most XT-disk controllers, some tape-backup controllers, SCSI disk controllers (including CD-ROM controllers), Adlib and Sound Blaster sound boards, Microsoft InPort mouse board
6	Floppy-disk controllers
7	First parallel port (LPT1), tape-backup controllers, SCSI-disk controllers (including CD-ROM controllers), Adlib and Sound Blaster sound boards

I/O ADDRESS	DEVICE
1F0h	XT hard-disk controllers
220h	3270 emulation boards, Adlib and Sound Blaster sound boards
240h	Hewlett-Packard scanners, some CD-ROM interface boards
278h	Second parallel port (LPT2)
280h	Tape-backup controllers
2E8h	Serial port COM4
3E8h	Serial port COM3
2F8h	Serial port COM2
3F8h	Serial port COM1
3F0h	Floppy-disk controller
378h	First parallel port (LPT1)
3B0h	Mono, EGA, and VGA video boards
3C0h	EGA and VGA video boards
3D0h	CGA and MCGA video boards

Problems will arise if your network board attempts to use the same I/O port addresses, memory addresses, or interrupt request lines used by other components already in your system. When this happens, one or both of the conflicting devices won't operate. This may cause you to learn more about the inner workings of your PC than you ever wanted to. The more expansion options you have in your PC, the more likely you are to encounter a conflict.

Depending on the type of network board you are using, you'll have to select an I/O port address, a memory address, an IRQ line, and, possibly, a DMA channel to use for the operation of the board. If you are using a board with an on-board boot ROM, you'll also need to select an address for the boot ROM.

Understanding I/O and Memory Addressing

All network interface boards fall into one of two groups: I/O mapped or memory mapped. These two groups define how the computer's CPU communicates with the board. In the case of I/O mapped boards, the board occupies several I/O port addresses on the CPU's I/O bus, much like a serial or parallel port. Data coming from the network appears to the computer's CPU as a stream of data coming in one of the I/O addresses; data being sent to the network is sent to another, usually adjacent I/O address. Memory-mapped boards are similar, but use a reserved area of the PC's main memory instead of I/O ports.

Neither method is inherently better than the other. Memory-mapped operation is somewhat faster than I/O mapped operation, but the memory on a memory-mapped card usually occupies some of the precious below-640K low-DOS memory. Most newer network boards are I/O mapped, but you can still use a memory-mapped board with Windows.

Some professional network installers consider the techniques they use to avoid interrupt and memory address conflicts as trade secrets, but the real secret is organization. Knowing the I/O and interrupt addresses used in each machine can avoid frustration and save hours of installation time.

The first piece of advice we can give you about network adapter installation is to use the defaults recommended by the manufacturer of the adapter. The manufacturer chose those defaults to avoid typical problems. If the adapter doesn't work at the default memory and/or I/O address, the board's installation manual typically lists at least two alternative settings. Adapters designed for the standard IBM PC/AT expansion bus (the Industry Standard Architecture or ISA bus) usually use jumpers or switches to determine the shared RAM address and IRQ line. Adapters designed for the Microchannel Architecture (MCA) and Extended Industry Standard Architecture (EISA) change all parameters through special configuration programs provided on a floppy disk shipped with the adapter.

One important point to remember: If you change the board's settings, you must reconfigure your network software to match the address and IRQ set on the board. The software can't find the adapter if it doesn't know where to look.

Selecting Interrupt Request (IRQ) Lines

Virtually all network boards use one of the PC's interrupt request (IRQ) lines. An *interrupt* is a signal sent to the CPU to indicate that a particular piece of hardware or software requires the CPU's immediate attention.

The first installation tip you should know concerns interrupt request line IRQ3. The COM2 serial port on all PCs uses this IRQ line. However, many LAN adapters come with this same IRQ line set as the default. If you install a LAN adapter using IRQ3 in a PC with a COM2 port, the serial port will probably stop working. If you have a modem or serial mouse attached to COM2, and the modem or mouse doesn't work when you're logged in to the network, you probably have this problem. Try moving the network adapter to another IRQ line; see Table 3.1.

If you don't need the COM2 port, you probably can disable it. Many manufacturers of PCs provide a method in either software or hardware to disable an on-board COM2 port, but there is no standard technique.

Because so many IBM PC/AT clones come equipped with a COM2 port, many installers avoid using IRQ3 and, instead, use IRQ5 when they install LAN adapters in these computers. But don't try this setting in an older IBM PC/XT or clone because the hard-disk controller in an XT will conflict with IRQ5 every time. Similarly, the LPT2 parallel port also uses interrupt line IRQ5. As with the COM2 port, most PC vendors provide a way to disable the LPT2 port if you don't need it.

Selecting IRQ2 for the LAN adapter usually works on AT-class machines. However, this IRQ line is used to relay interrupt requests for IRQ lines 8 through 15, so you may encounter conflicts or performance degradation if any devices in the AT use these higher-numbered interrupts. IRQ2 conflicts often sneak up on you when you try to add an internal device to a PC that has been operating happily with a LAN adapter at IRQ2.

Some network boards allow selection of IRQ10 and IRQ15. These interrupt request lines aren't used in many PCs, and are a good choice if you're installing a board in a crowded PC.

Selecting an I/O and Memory Address

Due to the lack of industry standards, there are no hard and fast rules about which I/O port and memory addresses you can use. In most cases, the default

I/O port address (usually 300h to 340h) set by the manufacturer will probably work, unless you have another device installed at that address.

Memory-mapped network cards pose a different problem. These cards generally require 16 to 64K of address space in the PC's high-memory area. This area is also used by video boards, SCSI disk controllers, and other memory-mapped peripheral devices. Make sure that you don't install your network board set to the same address as an existing device.

A few LAN adapter boards use a technique called Direct Memory Access (DMA) to speed the transfer of data between the CPU and the network board. If you install an adapter using a DMA channel, try channel 3, 5, 6, or 7 on AT-style machines. On older XT-style machines, use DMA channel 2 to avoid conflicts with the XT's hard disk. However, all PCs use DMA2 for the floppy-drive controller, so someone trying to simultaneously use the floppy drive and a LAN adapter set to DMA2 may experience problems.

You usually won't have trouble setting up a LAN adapter in a typical client workstation if you use the default settings. However, the challenge comes when you want to put a LAN adapter in a PC equipped with a special adapter for a mainframe connection or with a tape-drive controller. These devices and, to a lesser extent, internal mouse adapters often default to the same IRQ and memory locations used by LAN adapters. Some conflicts are insidious. For example, you might not see a problem until you try to back up the tape and pull files across the network at the same time. In this case, one of the conflicting products must move to a different address and/or IRQ line.

Getting multiple boards to work together in tricky installations is often a matter of experience and luck. That's why many system integrators support only product lines proven to be able to work together. LAN installation is, in some sense, an art, but it's primarily a skill with specific rules and a road map of the PC's architecture for you to follow.

■ Windows for Workgroups Installation

Before you install the Windows for Workgroups software, there are a few more items to consider. First, you need to make sure that your system meets the requirements of Windows. Windows likes memory: Windows for Workgroups requires at least 4MB of memory as an absolute minimum; 6 MB is a more realistic minimum. You'll also need memory-management software compatible with Microsoft's XMS standard and with the LIM EMS 4.0 standard. Windows includes an XMS-compatible memory manager, HIMEM.SYS, but you can use QEMM, 386MAX, or any other compatible memory-management program.

Besides memory, you'll need some disk space—about 12 to 14MB of it. Windows can run from your local hard disk, from a network file server, or from a combination of the two. Before we discuss the specifics of the installation process, you will need to decide which of the following three methods is best for your installation.

Local Hard-Disk Installation   If you have a local hard disk, then you can and should run Windows entirely from the hard disk. Windows's performance is at its best when running from a locally attached hard disk. The downside to this method is that a typical Windows installation will take about 12 to 14MB of local disk space.

All-Network Installation   If you are using a diskless workstation on a NetWare or LAN Manager network and don't have a local hard disk, you must run Windows entirely from the network. There are several disadvantages to this approach. First, all of the Windows program code must load from the server. Since Windows is very disk intensive, this will increase the amount of traffic on the network.

Second, Windows running on 386 and 486 systems creates a large workspace swap file when you start Windows. This file is typically 3 to 4MB in size, and is deleted when you exit from Windows. This process takes a noticeable amount of time, even with a fast 386 system on a lightly loaded network.

NOTE. *Unnecessary network traffic is every system administrator's number 1 enemy. Several diskless workstations running Windows from the network can create a network traffic jam. If you have a diskless 386 or 486 workstation, we strongly suggest that you set up a large RAM drive and use it as your swap drive.*

Mixed Local/Network Installation   If you have a local hard disk but don't want to give up the disk space required by Windows, you can install Windows to load from a network file server. Using this method, Windows installs only a minimal amount of data (about 250K) on your local hard disk; the remainder of Windows is loaded from a shared directory on the network. Performance with this method is nearly as good as running entirely from the hard disk. The downside is that the bulk of your Windows program code must travel over the network, thus increasing network traffic.

No matter which of the three installation options you choose, be sure to make a backup copy of your CONFIG.SYS and AUTOEXEC.BAT files before you begin. As we'll see later, the SETUP program may make some unwanted changes to these files.

If you already have Windows 3.0 or 3.1 installed on your PC, the Windows for Workgroups installation process will automatically update your existing Windows installation to Windows for Workgroups. We were skeptical about this feature at first, but test installations on several machines showed that the update process works as promised. Our existing Windows 3.0 and 3.1 machines were updated to Windows for Workgroups, and our existing desktop arrangement, special WIN.INI settings, and other customized options were left intact.

Installing Windows for Workgroups on Your Local Hard Disk

There are no special tricks for installing Windows on your local hard disk. If you are installing Windows for the first time, load your existing network software before you install Windows. Put the Windows Disk 1 in the A or B drive, and run the Windows SETUP program. If your network software is loaded when you run SETUP, the SETUP program will recognize the network hardware and software, and it will automatically configure Windows to work with your existing network.

The SETUP program will ask you to insert the nine installation floppy disks in order. The installation process takes between 30 and 60 minutes, depending on the speed of your PC and the number of options you install.

Installing Windows for Workgroups from a File Server

If your organization has an existing LAN Manager or NetWare network, you can install Windows from the network. This process allows you to keep a master copy of Windows on a file server and then install individual workstations from the master copy. To create the master copy, you run SETUP with the /A (administrative) option. SETUP will prompt you to insert each of the Windows floppy disks. As you insert the floppy disks, SETUP copies the files onto the server's hard disk.

There are two ways to use the master copy of Windows. First, you can use the master copy instead of the original Windows floppy disks to perform a complete local installation of Windows on any workstation on the network. We've found this method very convenient to use, since you don't have to insert and remove the Windows floppy disk over and over again. To use this option, follow these steps:

1. Install the master Windows files onto a server with the SETUP/A command.

2. Go to the workstation(s) where you want to install Windows and map a drive to the server that contains the master Windows files.

3. Run SETUP from the shared Windows directory.

After SETUP is finished, you'll have a complete copy of Windows on the workstation, just as if you had installed Windows from the floppy disks.

The second method allows you to create a Windows installation where most or all of Windows loads from the network. Under this method, the SETUP program copies a few essential files to the workstation hard disk or to a private directory on a server. The bulk of the Windows program files load from the shared directory on the server. This solution works well if your workstations don't have enough free disk space (about 11MB) for the full Windows installation. To use this option, follow these steps:

1. Install the master Windows files onto a server with the SETUP/A command as described above.

2. Go to the workstation where you want to install Windows and map a drive to the server that contains the master Windows files. If you're using a diskless workstation, create another drive mapping to contain your personal Windows files.

3. Run SETUP with the /N option from the shared Windows directory. SETUP will copy only the necessary Windows files to your local hard disk or network directory.

When you run Windows, it will start from your personal directory or local hard disk, and will load the bulk of the Windows program code from the shared network-installation directory.

Windows for Workgroups, CONFIG.SYS, and AUTOEXEC.BAT

During the installation process, Windows will modify your CONFIG.SYS and AUTOEXEC.BAT files. Most of the changes are necessary for the proper operation of Windows for Workgroups, but SETUP will often make changes you don't want or need. For this reason, you should always make a backup copy of your CONFIG.SYS and AUTOEXEC.BAT files before you run SETUP. The SETUP program automatically makes backup copies of these files, but it can't hurt to have an extra copy.

The most important change SETUP makes to CONFIG.SYS is the addition of commands to load several device drivers. These device drivers provide support for your network hardware and software. Table 3.2 shows some typical CONFIG.SYS device-driver commands.

In most cases, SETUP changes CONFIG.SYS to install the HIMEM.SYS and EMM386.EXE memory-management software. If you are using another memory manager (such as QEMM or 386Max), you do not need or want to install HIMEM and EMM386.

If SETUP thinks you need more DOS file handles or disk buffers, then SETUP will change the FILES and BUFFERS statements in your CONFIG.SYS file. If you are using a third-part memory-manager program such as QEMM, Netroom, or 386MAX, it is possible that those programs are already increasing your files and buffers.

Table 3.2

SETUP automatically adds these commands to your CONFIG.SYS file

COMMAND IN CONFIG.SYS	PURPOSE
device=c:\windows\protman.dos /i:c:\windows	Loads the Windows for Workgroups protocol manager. The /I: option tells PROTMAN.DOS where to find the PROTOCOL.INI file, which contains detailed information about your network hardware and software.
device=C:\WINDOWS\workgrp.sys	Loads the WORKGRP.SYS file and printer sharing driver.
device=C:\WINDOWS\ne2000.dos	Loads a device driver for your specific network board; in this case, a Novell NE-2000. This line will vary depending on the type of network board installed in your PC.
device=C:\WINDOWS\msipx.sys	Loads support for the Novell IPX protocol. This line is added only if your PC is part of a NetWare network.

The SETUP program also makes some changes to AUTOEXEC.BAT. In all cases, SETUP adds the command NET START to load and start the Windows for Workgroups redirector program. If your PC is on a NetWare network, SETUP also adds the commands MSIPX and NETX to your AUTOEXEC.BAT file. These two commands load the IPX protocol driver and the NetWare shell program. We'll examine the Workgroups-NetWare connection in detail in Chapter 7.

When Things Go Wrong . . .

The Windows SETUP program does a remarkable job of customizing Windows to fit your system. Unfortunately, given the huge number of PC types, network boards, video boards, operating systems, and other variables, it's possible for many things to go wrong. If Windows isn't installed properly, your system may exhibit any number of unpleasant behaviors. In extreme cases, the SETUP program itself may be unable to run or may crash partway through the installation process.

Because so much can go wrong, it can be very difficult to track down the problem. A few useful pointers are discussed below.

Start simple. If your system has many options (CD-ROM drive, removable hard disk, sound board, etc.), try un-installing any drivers for those devices before you run the SETUP program. In most cases, you'll need to edit CONFIG.SYS and/or AUTOEXEC.BAT to remove the commands that load the drivers. Make sure that you keep a backup copy of your existing CONFIG.SYS and AUTOEXEC.BAT, preferably on a floppy disk.

If Windows installs correctly with the additional drivers removed, add the drivers one at a time until you track down the culprit. In some cases, you may need to obtain new drivers that are compatible with Windows 3.1. The SETUP.TXT file installed in your Windows directory lists programs and hardware that are known to be incompatible with Windows for Workgroups 3.1.

If you have installed a virus protection program on your PC, remove or turn off the program before you attempt to run SETUP.

Don't trust third-party Windows drivers. Many video boards, particularly "accelerated" graphics boards, come with their own Windows screen drivers. If you're using one of these boards, install Windows for a plain vanilla VGA or 8514 video adapter, and make sure everything works before you install the drivers for your video board. Most of these drivers require changes to the WIN.INI and SYSTEM.INI system configuration files. When you attempt to install the hardware-specific video drivers, make backup copies of the WIN.INI and SYSTEM.INI files so that you can return your system to a normal configuration if something goes wrong while installing the drivers.

If your PC contains a memory-mapped network board, you may need to tell Windows to avoid using the memory area occupied by the video board. This is done by adding a line to your SYSTEM.INI file. See Chapter 11 for more details on SYSTEM.INI.

If you're using a third-party memory manager like QEMM or 386MAX, you may need an updated version of the memory-management software. Remove your memory manager and let SETUP install HIMEM.SYS and EMM386 instead. If Windows runs correctly with HIMEM and EMM386, contact your memory-management vendor for an update.

Similarly, third-party disk-cache programs can cause problems with Windows, particularly on 386 and 486 systems. Windows includes a disk-cache program, SMARTRV.EXE, which was designed to work in conjunction with Windows. If SMARTDRV works and your own cache program doesn't, contact your software vendor for an updated version of the cache program.

If you're running Windows on a removable hard disk (SyDOS or Bernoulli) or on a disk compressed with a disk-compression program such as STACKER, make sure that the commands to load your external disk driver or compression program appear in CONFIG.SYS and/or AUTOEXEC.BAT before the Windows network-driver commands.

- *So What Does It Do?*
- *Using and Sharing Disks and Printers*
- *Using the Chat Program*
- *Network Etiquette*

CHAPTER

Windows for Workgroups Basics

THIS CHAPTER WILL SHOW YOU HOW TO PERFORM THE FOUR BASIC Windows for Workgroups networking operations: (1) connect to a shared disk on another PC, (2) share files on your disk with other users, (3) use a shared printer on another PC, and (4) share your printer with other users. First, we'll give you a broad view of computer networking and then we'll examine specifically the capabilities of Windows for Workgroups.

■ So What Does It Do?

Like all networking software, Windows for Workgroups allows users on the network to use shared resources. As with most other networks, those resources fall into two general categories: shared disks and shared printers.

The networking software built into Windows for Workgroups is a *peer-to-peer network*. In essence, this means that any machine on the network can provide shared resources for others to use, and every machine can use shared resources provided by others. For example, if your PC has an expensive color laser printer and Jill's PC has a 1-gigabyte hard disk, you can use some of the space on Jill's hard disk and Jill can use your laser printer.

Other networks called *server-based networks* allow users to share disks and printers, too. But in a server-based LAN, all the shared resources must reside on a dedicated PC—the server. Novell's NetWare is the classic example of a server-based network. A typical NetWare network consists of one or more file servers and any number of client PCs. Each server can control several shared disks and several shared printers. A NetWare network may contain multiple servers; we've seen NetWare LANs with as many as 50. Figure 4.1 shows a typical NetWare network with one server and several workstations.

Server-based networks impose a rigid hierarchy on the network: Shared resources reside on a server, and that's that. An inherent problem with this rigidity is that there's no easy way to move files between client PCs. To move a file from one PC to another, you must first copy the file to a shared disk on the server. In most network environments, both the sending and receiving user must have permission to use the same directory or shared disk on the server—a requirement that's often difficult to arrange. We've seen employees in well-networked organizations running floppy disks between offices because they can't exchange files across the $100,000 network!

Windows for Workgroups lets you have the best of both worlds. The peer-to-peer networking is an inherent part of Windows for Workgroups, and Windows for Workgroups integrates well with NetWare and LAN Manager server-based networks. Your PC can be a client to a NetWare or LAN Manager network and can also act as a Windows for Workgroups server and/or client—all at the same time. We'll take a close look at interoperation with LAN Manager and NetWare in Chapter 7.

Besides the obvious advantages of sharing files and printers, there are other benefits to networking your PCs. When you connect all of your PCs into a network, you create a digital pipeline between each of them. Typically, you use this pipeline (we like to call it a "data hose") to move files and print data between PCs on the network. But the same connections that make machine-to-machine communications more effective can also make person-to-person communications flow better as well. The Windows for Workgroups package includes three features designed to improve interpersonal communications in your office: a network electronic-mail program, a network scheduling program, and a network Chat program. We'll look at Mail and Schedule+ in Chapters 5 and 6, and we'll examine Chat later in this chapter.

Figure 4.1

This is an example of a Novell NetWare server-based network. In the world of server-based networking, all shared resources must reside on a dedicated PC called a server. The attached client PCs can use any of the disk or printer resources available on the server.

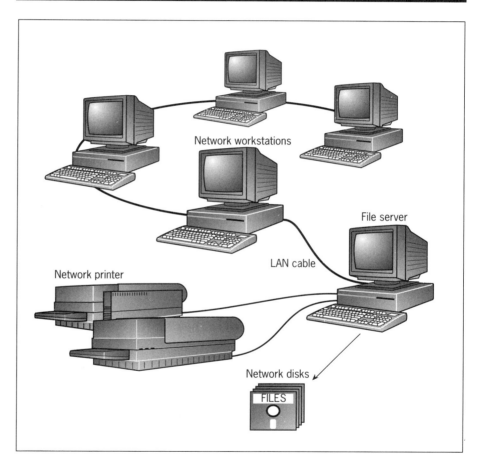

In the next two sections, we'll show you how to make disk and printer resources available for others to use and how to use resources on other PCs. We'll assume that you're familiar with basic Windows operations such as starting a program, using the mouse, and printing a document. If you're not up to speed on Windows itself, this would be a good time to take a break from this book and spend some time with the Windows user's guide or with *PC Magazine Guide to Using Windows 3.1* by Gus Venditto.

■ Using and Sharing Disks and Printers

As we saw earlier, Windows for Workgroups allows users to share resources over the network. When you connect your PC to a shared disk, you choose an unused drive letter (for example, F or Z) to assign to the network resource. There's nothing fundamentally different about the files on the shared disk—except that the actual magnetic 1s and 0s that make up the disk are located on someone else's desktop. Similarly, network printers appear in your list of available printers just like local printers do. Again, the only difference is that the printer is located elsewhere in the building.

You control network disks through the File Manager, and you control network printers with the Printers module of the Control Panel and with the Print Manager. The following table shows which program to use for each of the four basic networking operations:

To Do This:	Use This:
Connect to a shared disk	File Manager
Share your disk with other users	File Manager
Connect to a shared printer	Printers module of the Control Panel or Print Manager
Share your printer with other users	Control Panel (to set up printer); Print Manager (to share printer)

In the following sections, we'll take a close look at each of the above operations. In order to share disks and printers with other users, your PC must have an 80386 or higher CPU, and Windows must be running in 386-Enhanced mode. Windows automatically starts in Enhanced mode if your PC has an 80386 or 80486 with more than 3 megabytes of extended memory. If your PC has less than 3 megabytes of extended memory or an 80286 CPU, Windows will start in Standard mode. See the Windows user's guide for more information on Standard and Enhanced mode operation.

Using a Shared Disk

Your PC probably has a floppy disk designated as drive A:, and a hard disk designated drive C:. These are real, physical disk drives; they really exist in your computer. In addition, Windows for Workgroups allows you to use disk drives on someone else's computer; these *logical* drives appear on your PC with such names as F: or X:. The Windows for Workgroups software essentially tricks DOS into thinking that it has another disk drive or two.

To the user on a client PC, a Windows for Workgroups network drive appears very much like a regular DOS drive. Windows for Workgroups drives have volume names, as do DOS drives; and Windows for Workgroups volumes have subdirectories, and subdirectories contain individual files, as do DOS disks.

Access Privileges

For all the similarities to regular DOS disks, there are also major differences between a logical network drive and a physical drive.

If you have a hard disk on your PC, you have access to all the files on that hard disk. You are free to view files, create files, delete files, change existing files, or even to format the entire hard disk. On a network drive, you may or may not have any of these rights. File- and printer-access privileges are controlled by the owner of the PC where the resource resides. The owner may choose to password-protect the shared directories. If you don't know the password, you can't use the shared directory.

File Sharing and Record Locking

There is another difference between network disks and your PC's physical disks. On a network, it is possible for more than one user to have access to the same file at the same time. This doesn't normally happen on a non-networked PC, since only one user can use the PC at a time. If all the users are only reading the file on the network disk, there is no problem; all the users see the same data. However, if more than one user tries to write to the same file at the same time, there is obviously a potential for conflict. To prevent conflicts caused by many users trying to write to the same file at once, Windows for Workgroups uses the record-locking mechanism built into DOS version 3.1 and higher. Record locking allows the network to block access to a portion of a file while a user writes data to the file.

Connecting to a Shared Disk

Before you can use a shared disk, you must establish a connection between your PC and the PC providing the shared-disk resource. You make connections to remote disks with the File Manager program.

To connect to a shared disk on another networked PC, follow these steps:

1. Start the File Manager by double-clicking on the File Manager icon.

2. Click on the Connect Network Drive icon (▦), or select Connect Network Drive from the *Disk* menu. Windows will display the Connect Network Drive dialog box.

3. Select the drive letter to use from the Drive drop-down list at the top of the dialog box. You may also type the drive letter to use. If the drive

letter is already in use, Windows will display the connection name assigned to the drive letter.

4. Select a workgroup from the list of available Workgroups. Click on the desired workgroup to see the available servers in the workgroup. Figure 4.2 shows a server display with several servers in one workgroup.

Figure 4.2

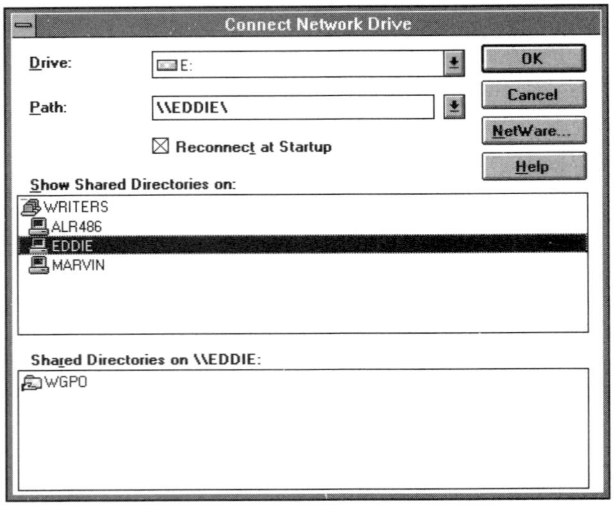

The File Manager's display of available servers is shown here. In this example, there are three servers available in the Workgroup named Writers.

5. Click on the desired machine name. A list of available shared disks will appear in the lower portion of the window.

6. If you want Windows to automatically restore this connection each time you start Windows, click the Reconnect at Startup box.

7. If the selected directory is password protected, you'll be asked to enter the password. If you want Windows to store the password for future use, select the box marked Save this Password.

8. Click on the OK box to establish the new drive connection.

If you know the full server and directory name of the shared disk, you can streamline this process by typing the full path name (for example \\EDDIE\WINWORD\DOCS) in the Path setting and clicking on OK.

You can create as many drive connections as you need, using the available drive letters up to Z:. To disconnect a shared drive, select the Disconnect icon ( ), or select Disconnect Network Drive from the File Manager's Disk menu. Select the drive to disconnect, and click on OK.

Sharing Your Disk

Before another user can access your disk or printer, you must explicitly make the printer or the directory available for others to use. This may seem an inconvenience, but you probably don't want to make your entire hard disk and your printer available to everyone on the network.

Sharing and Security

Because Windows for Workgroups is so easy to set up and use, many users overlook one important fact: Networks must be managed. We're not saying that a three-user network needs to have a full-time network administrator, but even small networks need occasional attention.

The old adage about too many cooks spoiling the broth still holds true in the information age. As your network grows larger, it becomes harder to manage. We've found that it's usually best to designate one person or a small group of people as the primary network manager(s). That person or persons should have responsibility for setting up and maintaining a master list of shared network devices, making backups of network files, and installing new software on the network.

One of the main reasons that companies install networks is to promote fast and convenient data sharing. As a network manager, you must make sure that your users have access to that data. And this brings up the issue of data security. Even the smallest company is likely to have sensitive or confidential data stored on one or more PCs on the network. Keeping private data private is an essential element of good network management.

Like all networking systems, Windows for Workgroups provides some security measures designed to keep data private. When you start Windows for Workgroups for the first time, you'll be asked to enter your user name and to choose a password. This name and password identifies you to the other PCs on the network. Windows stores the name and password on your disk so that it can identify you the next time you start Windows.

Each shared disk resource may have one or two optional passwords assigned to it. One password allows full read and write access to the resource, and the second password allows read-only access. When a user attempts to connect to a password-protected shared disk, he or she will be asked to enter the password for the resource. If the user can't supply one of the passwords, then the access request is denied. Similarly, each shared printer can have an associated password. Users must know the password before they can use the printer.

As you connect to new shared resources, Windows makes a note of your password for each of the shared devices in a special password file on your hard disk. The next time you connect to a resource, Windows will automatically provide the password you entered the first time you connected to the resource. If the password has been changed, you'll be prompted to enter the new password. Microsoft calls this very convenient feature *password caching*. In case you're wondering, the passwords are stored in the same file as the user name and password that you use to start Windows. The data file itself is encrypted so that other users can't read through your password file and learn the passwords stored in it. The user name and password you supply at Windows start-up time is essentially the master key to the rest of your passwords.

Setting Up a Shared Disk

To allow access to a directory on your disk, follow these steps:

1. Start the File Manager by double-clicking on the File Manager icon.

2. Select the directory you want to share. If you want to share your entire C drive, click the C icon at the top of the directory structure.

3. Click the Share icon (📂), or select Share As from the File Manager's Disk menu. You'll see a dialog box like the one in Figure 4.3.

Figure 4.3

In this example, we're preparing to share the C directory, which allows other users access to the entire disk.

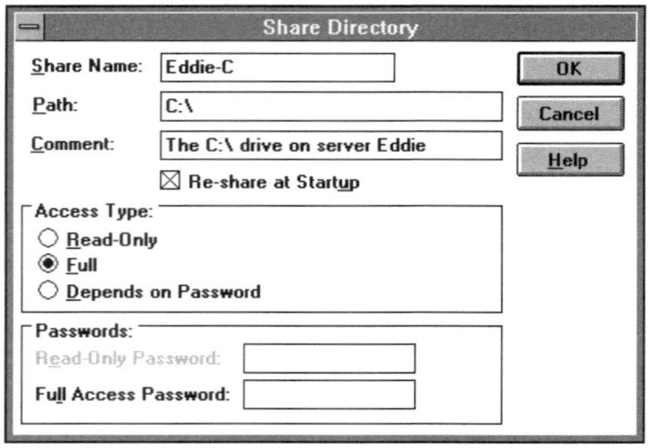

The Share Directory dialog box contains several settings that affect the way other users can use the shared disk:

- *Share Name* specifies the name, up to 12 characters long, that others will see when they connect to your disk.

- *Path* specifies the actual pathname of the shared directory. In our example, we used C:\, the root directory on the C drive. If you specify an explicit directory name, you can restrict access to only the files in the directory. For example, sharing the files in C:\WINDOWS\GAMES allows other users to use the files in \WINDOWS\GAMES, but does not allow access to any other directories. To share multiple subdirectories without sharing your entire hard disk, you must explicitly share each individual subdirectory.

- *Comment* contains an optional field—up to 48 characters—that describes the contents of the shared directory. Other users will see this comment when they browse through the available resources list.

- *Re-share at Startup* tells Windows whether this is permanent or temporary share. If this box is checked, Windows will automatically re-share this directory the next time you start Windows for Workgroups—a permanent share. If the box is not checked, then the directory will be shared only until you exit from Windows.

- The three fields in the Access Type box determine the amount of access other users have to the shared directory. *Read-Only* specifies that other users may read data from the files, but that they may not create new files, delete files, or change the contents of any files. *Full* allows users full access to the directory; they can delete, modify, and create new files in the subdirectory. *Depends on Password* allows either read-only or full access, depending on the password provided by the user. This allows you to permit full access to some users and restrict others to read-only status.

- The Passwords box contains two passwords: one for *Read-Only* access (dimmed in Figure 4.3 because we have specified Full access), and one for *Full Access*. The passwords may be up to eight characters long, and are not case sensitive.

After you fill in the fields and click the OK box, the directory is immediately available to other users on the network. As a reminder, the File Manager directory displays shared folder with a different icon than private folders. A normal, unshared folder appears as a plain manila folder icon, and a shared folder appears as a manila folder with a hand beneath it. Figure 4.4 shows a File Manager display with several shared folders.

Once you've created one or more shared directories, your PC begins to function as a file server. This process is completely transparent; you don't have to do anything special to make your shared files available to other users. In most cases, you won't be able to tell when other users are connected to your PC and using your shared disk resources. In Chapter 11, we'll show you how to use the NetWatcher and WinMeter programs to monitor network activity.

Sharing Printers

Network printing can be a thing of wonder. When it's set up and working correctly, you can click the Print menu in your application, walk to the shared printer, and pick up a perfectly formatted, crisply printed document. When it's not working, it can be a major source of frustration. In this section, we'll show you how to have more of the former and less of the latter.

Figure 4.4

The main File Manager directory display is shown here. The directories with the 📁 icon are shared directories.

Shared folders

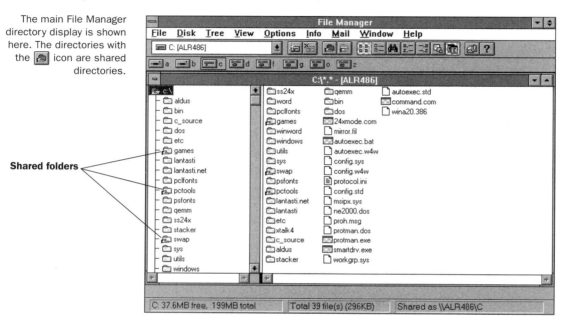

Before you can use or share a printer, you must make sure that you have the proper printer driver installed on your PC. Every different make and model of printer requires its one unique printer driver. The Windows for Workgroups retail package includes hundreds of printer drivers, and many printer manufacturers include a Windows driver disk in the box with their printers. If you try to print with the wrong driver, you'll encounter all sorts of problems—more on this later.

When you install Windows, the SETUP program asks you to choose your printer or printers from a long list of supported printer types. SETUP then copies the necessary printer drivers to your Windows system directory. If you installed Windows for one type of printer and want to use a different type of printer over the network, you'll need to install an additional printer driver. Before you can install the printer driver, you'll need to know the exact make and model of the network printer you want to use. If the network printer is a laser printer, you'll also need to know how much memory is installed in the printer.

Although SETUP allows you to select more than one printer, only one printer may be active at one time. If you're connected to a network with several different types of printers, you'll need to install the printer drivers for each printer you intend to use.

You install printer drivers with the Printers icon in the Windows Control Panel. On a stand-alone PC, the Printers module of the Control Panel selects the type of printer you have, and tells Windows which printer port to use. In a network environment, the Printers module also tells Windows which of the available network printers to use.

The printer selection process can be somewhat confusing, since Windows will allow you to connect any local printer type to any network printer. For example, Windows will allow you to connect your HP printer driver to a PostScript printer on another machine. If you do this, you'll encounter all types of strange problems because the target printer won't understand the data being sent by your PC. The good news is that once you get it right, Windows remembers your printer settings between Windows sessions.

Connecting to a Shared Printer

Connecting to a network printer is a two-part process. First you must install the necessary printer driver, and then you can establish a connection from your PC to the shared printer.

To install a new printer driver, follow these steps:

1. From the Windows desktop, open the Control Panel by double-clicking on the Control Panel icon. Select the Printers module by double-clicking on the Printers icon.

2. Check the list of installed printers. If the printer you want to use appears in the list, you're ready to use the shared printer.

3. Click on the Add >> button. Windows will display a list of all the standard printer drivers, as shown in Figure 4.5.

4. Select your printer from the list of printers, and click the Install button. Windows will ask you insert a disk containing the printer driver. Windows will copy the driver file to your hard disk. The newly installed printer driver should then appear in the Installed Printers list at the top of the window.

You can connect your PC to a network printer from the Printers module of the Control Panel, or from the Print Manager program. To connect a network printer from the Control Panel, follow these steps:

1. Select the desired printer driver in the Installed Printers list, and click on the Connect button, then click the Network button.

2. Select a server from the list of network servers in the middle of the window. When you click on a server, the printers attached to the server will appear in the lower window.

3. Select a printer and click the OK button.

Figure 4.5

Choose a printer from the List of Printers to install the corresponding driver.

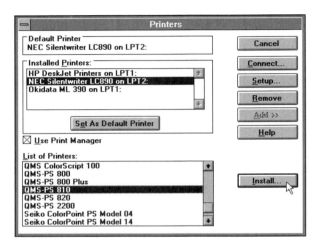

To connect to a network printer from the Print Manager, follow these steps:

1. Start the Print Manager program by double-clicking on the Print Manager icon from the Windows desktop.

2. Select Connect Network Printer from the *Printer* pull-down menu, or click on the Connect Network Printer icon ( ).

3. Select a server from the list of network servers in the middle of the window (see Figure 4.6). When you click on a server, the shared printers attached to the server will appear in the lower portion of the window.

4. Select a printer from the Shared Printers list and click the OK button.

Although Windows allows you to install drivers for several printers, only one printer can be active at any given time. The active printer is called the *default printer*. You can select the default printer from the Control Panel or from the Print Manager.

To select a different default printer from the Control Panel, select the desired printer in the Printers module and then double-click the button Set As Default Printer. The new default printer setting will appear at the top of the window. To change the default printer from the Print Manager, select the desired printer in the list of printers, then click the Set Default Printer icon ( ), or select Set Default Printer from the Printer pull-down menu. The Print Manager displays the default printer in bold type in the printers display.

Figure 4.6

Connect to a network printer from the Printer Control Panel: The window in the middle of the screen shows the available servers, and the window at the bottom of the screen shows the printers available on the selected server. The Print Manager uses this same printer selection display.

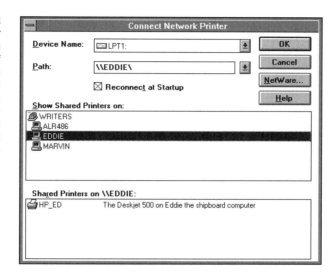

Some newer Windows applications let you select the printer from the application's File menu, and we hope that more software developers will follow suit. Unfortunately, most Windows application programs always use the default printer; there's no way to select a specific printer for a print job without first going to the Control Panel or Print Manager and selecting a different default printer.

Sharing Your Printer

Before you can share your printer, you should install the printer driver for your printer and make sure that the printer is installed, connected, and operating properly. Once you've determined that the printer is working correctly, you use the Print Manager program to make your printer available for sharing.

To share your printer, follow these steps:

1. Start the Print Manager program by double-clicking on the Print Manager icon from the Windows desktop.

2. Select the printer you wish to share.

3. Select Share Printer As from the Printer pull-down menu, or click on the Share Printer icon (🖨).

4. Fill in the information in the dialog box (see Figure 4.7). If you wish to share the printer each time you start Windows for Workgroups, click the Re-Share at Startup button.

Figure 4.7

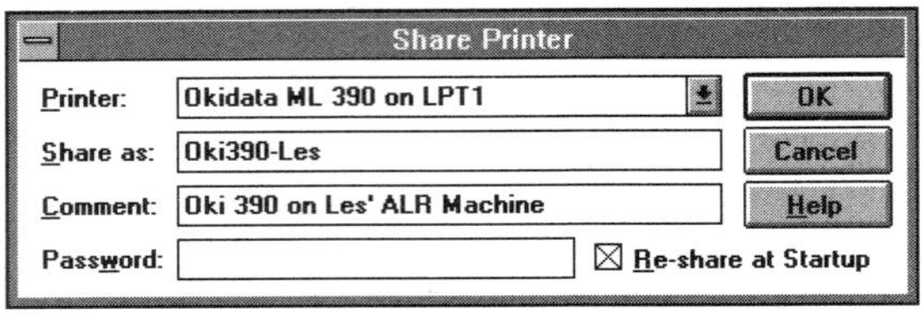

As shown by this Share Printer dialog box, we're sharing an Okidata 390 line printer with the share name OKI390-Les. This share name lets users know the exact make, model, and location of the printer. There's no password on this printer, so anyone on the network may use it.

5. Click the OK button.

As we pointed out earlier, you should give your printers descriptive share names. A good share name can indicate the make, model, and location of the shared printer. You can also use the Comment field to pass on any other information about the printer.

Some Printing Pointers

In many organizations, the initial motivation for installing a network comes from the need to share a few laser printers among many users. It's not difficult to share printers with Windows for Workgroups, but network printing requires close cooperation between Windows, your application programs, and the printer itself. It also requires a degree of coordination among the network users.

Network printing seems to be the one facet of networking that causes users a great deal of grief. Our experience has shown that nothing prints right the first time even on the printer attached directly to your PC. Using a networked printer can add another layer of frustration to your printing woes. When you use a shared network printer, you might send a big file to the printer, wait for the job to make its way through the printer queue behind print jobs from seven other people, and then find that the right margin is too wide, or that you printed it on the wrong type of paper or in the wrong typeface or format. You get the picture.

Here are a few simple but effective things you can do to avoid the most common network printing problems.

Review Your Print Job If your software provides a print preview feature, use it! Many word processor and spreadsheet packages have some sort of print preview function. Although you may not be able to see all the details of the document, most print previewers will let you see such glaring problems as bad pagination, wrong margins, and other formatting errors. Previewing saves time, effort, energy, paper, and printer ink, and prevents frustration!

Be Patient When you're using a shared printer, remember that you don't own the printer, even if that printer is attached to your PC! You are sharing the printer with several other users. If you are accustomed to printing on a printer directly attached to your PC, you expect the printer to start churning out paper as soon as you start printing. This is not so with network printers. When you send a print job to a network printer, there may be several other print jobs ahead of yours. The print jobs will normally print in the order they were received. In Chapter 11, we'll show you how to rearrange waiting print jobs.

Keep the Bins Stocked If you use more than one type of paper and your laser printer supports an optional second paper bin, buy it! Having two types of paper (plain and letterhead, for example) available at all times makes it easier for everyone, and reduces problems caused when users must change paper frequently. If you have a single-bin printer, always check the Print Manager to make sure no print jobs are waiting to print before you change paper.

Use the Right Printer Make sure that you are sending your print job to the right printer. If you've selected the PostScript printer driver from the Control Panel, then you must send your print job to a PostScript-compatible printer. If you send the job to a dot-matrix printer by mistake, you will get pages and pages of PostScript data on the line printer. Conversely, if you send a non-PostScript print job output to a PostScript printer, you will wait a very long time for nothing at all to happen. This is because PostScript printers do not print anything that is not sent to them in PostScript format! The printer will take the data, look at it, decide it's not PostScript, and ignore it.

A similar problem occurs frequently with Hewlett-Packard Laser-Jet printers. If you mistakenly send an HP print job to a dot-matrix printer, you may get only gibberish. This happens because the HP LaserJet printers use a series of control characters for special printer functions. For example, one frequently used control character means "eject the current page" to most dot-matrix printers.

■ Using the Chat Program

The Windows for Workgroups Chat program allows you to carry on a keyboard-to-screen "conversation" with another user on the network.

To call another user with the Chat program, double-click on the Chat icon from the Program Manager. Click on the Telephone Dial icon (🖳) or select Dial from the Conversation menu. You'll see the other PCs on the network listed by machine name. Select the machine you want to call, and click on the OK button.

When you receive an incoming chat request, the Chat icon will appear on your Windows desktop. If your PC is equipped with a Windows-compatible sound board, you'll hear the sound of a ringing telephone. To answer a chat request, double-click the Chat icon, or press Ctrl+Esc and select Chat from the Task List.

Once the chat session is established, each user's typing appears in one of the two windows on the screen. Figure 4.8 shows a chat session in progress.

Either user can end the chat session by clicking the Hang Up icon (🖳) or by selecting Hang Up from the Conversation menu.

Figure 4.8

This figure shows a network chat session in progress. Each user can see what the other is typing.

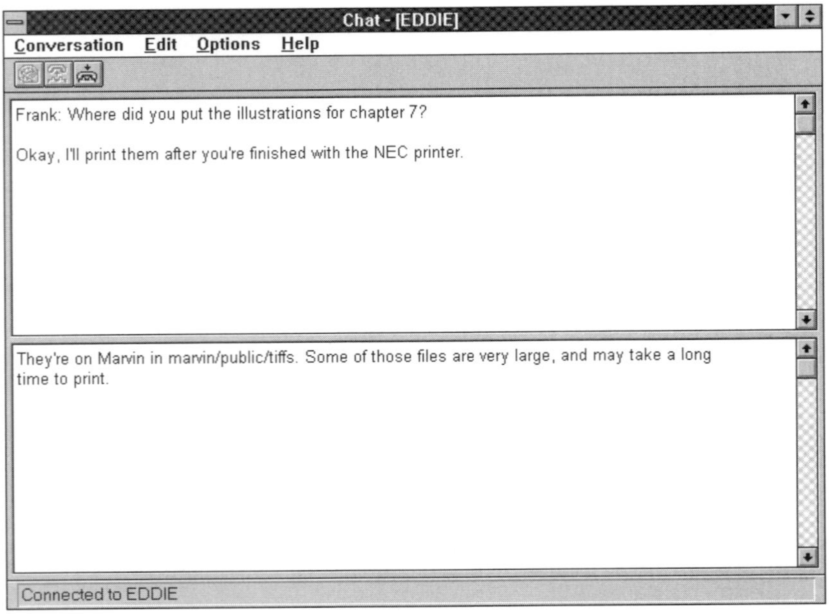

■ Network Etiquette

When your PC is providing shared disk or printer services for other users on the network, other users may rely on your PC for important work. In the interest of office-wide peace and harmony, here are a few pointers that can help prevent lost work:

- Never turn your PC off without exiting from Windows. When you exit from Windows via the Exit command on the File menu, Windows will warn you if other users are connected to your PC. If you simply shut the PC off without shutting down Windows, you'll never see the warning message, and other users on the network may lose their work or print jobs. In addition, Windows keeps many files open, especially on 386 and 486 systems. If you shut the PC off while Windows is writing to one of those files, you may damage the file structure on your hard disk.

- Don't close the Print Manager icon. Windows uses the Print Manager to manage print jobs from other users on the network. If your PC has a shared network printer attached, and you've told Windows to re-share your printer at startup, Windows will automatically load the Print Manager program each time you start Windows. The Print Manager program will appear as an icon on the Windows desktop display. If you close the Print Manager, your shared printer will not be available for others to use.

- Don't connect to printers and drives that you don't need. Network drive and printer connections utilize resources on the network. Every connection adds to the traffic on the network, and excessive traffic can slow the network to a crawl. You can help avoid the traffic jam by connecting only those printer and drive resources that you actually need to use. When you're finished with a network connection, close the connection.

- *Electronic Mail as a Workgroup Productivity Tool*
- *Electronic Mail Program Functions*
- *The Concept*
- *Installing Mail*
- *Placing the .MMF File*
- *Specifying Notification of Messages*
- *Making Mail*

- *Managing the Incoming Mail*
- *Managing the Mail System*

CHAPTER

5

Using the Electronic Mail

W<small>INDOWS FOR WORKGROUPS IS DIFFERENT FROM OTHER PEER-TO-</small>peer networking systems because of its emphasis on facilitating the workgroup process. Beyond the ability to simply share hard-disk drives and printers, the package contains two important engines that can power group activities: a slightly watered-down version of the Microsoft Mail electronic-mail system and the feature we call networked Distributed Data Exchange (DDE). We'll provide a hands-on guide to networked DDE in Chapter 8. In this chapter we'll describe how to set up and use the mail system in Windows for Workgroups, and in the next chapter we'll look at the first mail-powered application, Schedule+.

Workgroup productivity programs:

👍 Allow people to share information without disrupting the normal flow of work

👍 Provide time-saving and effort-saving ways to coordinate meetings and schedule the use of resources

👍 Allow people to discuss problems in real time without leaving their desks

👎 Require everyone to cooperate if they are to be effective

The definition of workgroup productivity software is pretty simple: LAN-based software that makes people more productive as a group. These products, which generally fall into the categories of scheduling, project management, and document control, all benefit from having an underlying electronic-mail system ready to carry information between users. Electronic mail is the core of workgroup productivity. In the ideal case, workgroup productivity programs use the power of the network to help people work together more effectively, improve efficiency, and decrease the time needed to do important, but sometimes irritating tasks.

■ Electronic Mail as a Workgroup Productivity Tool

For most of recorded history, you couldn't engage in real-time communications farther than you could project your voice. The time needed to communicate severely limited the quantity and quality of the communications. The introduction of electronic devices, particularly the telephone, eliminated the time needed to move messages across distances, but telephone communications brought with it the new time constraint of synchronicity—better known as telephone tag. For several decades of this century, if you didn't answer the phone when it rang, a potentially fast-moving message wasn't delivered.

We work around the problem of synchronization with voice mail and fax machines. Additionally, many organizations find relief from telephone tag and discover a whole new way of communicating through electronic mail. Electronic mail breaks the tyranny of time by moving messages across long distances quickly and by storing messages and forwarding them to you where and when you're ready to receive them.

Electronic-mail programs overlap with the telephone, overlap with face-to-face meetings, and also provide a method of communications all their own.

On a practical level, the biggest immediate benefit you get from using electronic mail is that it nearly eliminates telephone tag. The more people in an organization use e-mail, with its ability to store information and deliver it when the recipient is ready to take it, the less they are controlled by the tyranny of that real-time communications device, the telephone.

Although providing a means for out-of-sync communication is the most visible short-term benefit of electronic mail, the service has other longer-term attractions. More advanced systems such as Microsoft Mail include a special application program interface (API) that provides a way for other programs to link into the mail program. Through these links, the other applications learn the user names of people on the network and the names of the PCs they use to send messages—which may be much more than the typical few lines of text—to applications running on other networked PCs.

■ Electronic Mail Program Functions

E-mail programs:

👍 **Reduce telephone tag**

👍 **Improve efficiency**

👍 **Work with various computers and operating systems**

👍 **Span great distances**

👎 **Create complex installation problems**

The basic functions of electronic mail include creating, reading, forwarding, replying to, and providing receipts for messages. All e-mail packages must do these jobs. Of course, e-mail programs vary significantly in the utilities, menus, and other amenities they provide for creating and receiving messages.

Here are some of the most useful features in an e-mail system:

- Notification of incoming messages
- A text editor for message preparation
- An address book of users
- The ability to import text files into messages
- The ability to attach binary files to outgoing messages
- Return receipts for messages
- Electronic folders for special subjects
- Password protection of accounts

Electronic-mail programs running on mainframe and Unix-based computer networks defined these functions years ago. Microsoft's mail system included in Windows for Workgroups has all these functions.

Other e-mail features include the ability to set up special-interest bulletin boards where users can post messages pertaining to a specific topic, and in particular the ability to exchange messages with dissimilar mail systems. These functions are part of the larger Microsoft Mail package sold separately by Microsoft. Although the Mail program within Windows for Workgroups will work as a client for Microsoft Mail without change, you don't get bulletin boards or the ability to exchange electronic mail with systems outside of Windows for Workgroups without adding the larger Microsoft Mail system.

■ The Concept

The concept behind the electronic-mail system is simple: One networked PC makes a shared subdirectory available as a common mail storage depot to the other PCs on the network. The Mail program running in each PC regularly reads the shared subdirectory and checks for messages addressed to the name of the person logged in to the Mail program. Under the default settings, each Mail program checks with the Postoffice every 10 minutes, but you can adjust how often that happens. If a Mail program in a PC has an outgoing message, it deposits the message in the shared subdirectory where the appropriate program running on another PC picks it up.

Chapter 5: Using the Electronic Mail

The PC acting as the mail storage depot—Microsoft refers to this PC as the Postoffice, although it only has the passive role of storage rather than the active role of sorting and forwarding—must be a file server. Interestingly, the Postoffice doesn't have to be a Windows for Workgroups file server. It can be any file server running under any network operating system, including NetWare, as long as the client PCs have the proper networking software loaded to make use of that file server.

If the Postoffice is a Windows for Workgroups file server, it must run Windows in protected mode and have a hard-disk drive of a nominal size. We suggest 200MB minimum for all but the smallest offices.

■ Installing Mail

The software for the electronic-mail system loads automatically when you start the Setup program working from the first floppy in your Windows for Workgroups package. The Mail program appears as an icon in the Main window, as shown in Figure 5.1. You can, of course, move the program icon to any menu you wish simply by dragging and dropping it between windows.

Figure 5.1

Selecting the Mail icon in the Main window initiates the Mail program.

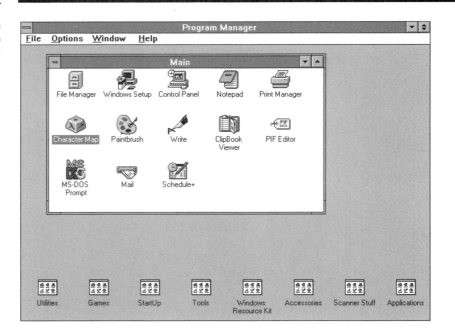

Double-clicking on the Mail icon starts the electronic mail program. If this is a new installation, you'll be given the option of creating a new Postoffice or opening an account at an existing one. Only one person in the workgroup should use the menu shown in Figure 5.2 to create a Postoffice. That person becomes the administrator of the Postoffice, so plan this action carefully. Keep in mind that as the amount of electronic mail activity grows the PC holding the Postoffice will spend a lot of time servicing network requests and have less capacity—in terms of processor speed and disk space—for local applications.

Figure 5.2

It is easy to designate a location for the Windows for Workgroups mail box. But make sure that the subdirectory, not just the drive root or any directory above the shared subdirectory, is shared.

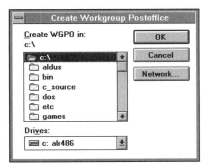

HINT. *Select a PC with a lot of disk storage and a low amount of local activity for the Postoffice. Also, make sure that it stays on during all working hours. This PC is as important as any network file server, and it deserves the protection of an uninterruptable power supply.*

The default name for the shared storage location for electronic mail is a subdirectory called WGPO. You must use File Manager to share WGPO with the other networked PCs, but note that you should share the WGPO subdirectory and not just the root directory above it. The shared subdirectory can be on any file server available through any networked drive.

Once you designate the shared subdirectory, you can either create the user names and passwords or allow each individual user to create a name and password for one new account.

HINT. *If only one person will sign on to electronic mail from each PC, then you can allow each person to create an individual user name and password through the Windows for Workgroups mail system. However, each program running on each PC will create a new user only once. If more than one person will sign on from a PC, the administrator must add that user's name and password to the mail system by selecting the Postoffice Manager option from the Mail pull-down menu in the Mail window.*

At each individual client PC, people use the menu shown in Figure 5.3 to select the shared Postoffice file. If you get the name of the shared subdirectory correct, this is a simple task.

Figure 5.3

Each person selects the desired shared subdirectory used as a Postoffice during the initial setup of the program. We recommend that everyone in the network use the same Postoffice unless you are very limited on disk-drive space.

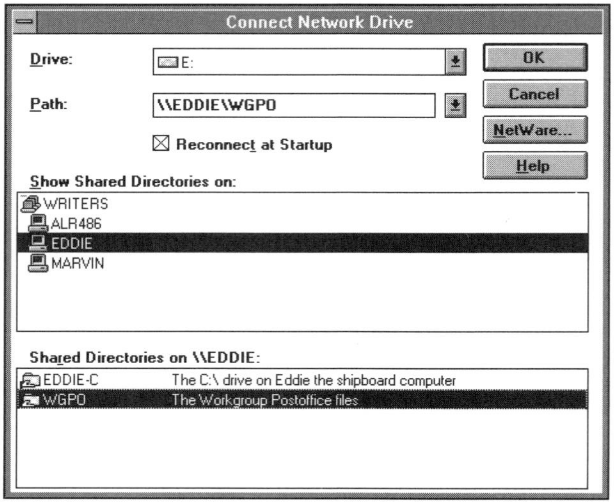

The program also prompts each new user for a name, mailbox, and password. The Name entry should be the person's full two-part name, but the Mailbox entry is limited to ten letters. The mailbox name in this window is an alias used by the electronic-mail program to identify a specific person.

In most organizations, people use their first initial and last name as the mailbox name, LFREED for example, but other groups use the first name and last initial, such as FRANKD. Either option or any other consistent naming method that you use will work with the program as long as the alias names don't exceed ten characters.

Unfortunately, Microsoft is inconsistent in what it calls the names people use for electronic mail. After the initial setup, anyone who chooses the Mail icon and starts Mail sees the login/password screen shown in Figure 5.4. Note that the Name entry requested in this prompt isn't the person's full name, but rather the alias of no more than ten letters. The confusion fades quickly, but initially the change in terms can cause the user to wonder which name to use. When in doubt, use the short name.

Figure 5.4

Every electronic mail user sees a standard login screen. The "Name" asked for in this screen is the short user alias of no more than ten letters.

The Mail program stores the information entered during the setup in a file called MSMAIL.INI in the Windows subdirectory. If you have problems getting into the Mail program, check to make sure that this file is in the correct subdirectory. The beginning of the file should look like this:

```
[Microsoft Mail]
WG=1
LocalMMF=1
NoServerOptions=1
DemosEnabled=0
ServerPath=D:\WGPO
CustomInitHandler=
Login=fderfler
OfflineMessages=C:\WINDOWS\MSMAIL.MMF
Window=15 59 629 445 1 1 1 0
```

In the sixth line, the term *ServerPath* points to the Postoffice file. In the eighth line, the term *Login* points to the short user name. Other standard lines in the file are not reproduced here.

HINT. *You can force Mail to start the setup process again if a new person takes over a PC or if there are errors in the initial setup. Simply erasing the MSMAIL.INI file in the \WINDOWS subdirectory fools the program into starting a new initialization sequence.*

■ Placing the .MMF File

The path for the MSMAIL.MMF file shown in the OfflineMessages= entry in MSMAIL.INI is very important. The .MMF file stores incoming and outgoing messages. If you will always log in from the same PC, then the .MMF file should reside on your local hard-disk drive. In this way you can manage its size as it consumes your storage space, always have access to it, keep it private, and avoid putting traffic on the network when you retrieve it. But if you will log in to the electronic-mail system from different networked PCs, you can't see the messages you have previously received or sent unless you can gain access to your .MMF file across the network.

In Chapter 9 we provide details on how to call into the network and access its resources using a telephone and a modem. You must consider your strategy carefully when you plan the location of the .MMF files for people who will call in from outside the network and for those who will use different networked PCs to check their mail.

You have three alternatives for placing an incoming caller's .MMF file: desktop storage, laptop storage, or mail server storage. None of these alternatives is ideal. You can choose to keep the .MMF file on your desktop PC and make it available across the network with a password. Your desktop PC must be turned on and available any time you dial into the network or use either of the access server alternatives described in Chapter 9. This is a good solution because it provides privacy and keeps the network load down, but you have to keep your PC on all the time.

Many modern laptop computers have a lot of processing power and storage. You can choose to make your laptop PC your main machine. You can attach it to the network through a modem when you are out of the office and use an external LAN adapter when you are in the office. This is an effective solution if you use the remote node type of remote access described in Chapter 9, but it doesn't work if you use the more common remote-control access scheme.

In any workgroup of more than a few people, you will want to keep the PC acting as a Postoffice running all the time. Because that machine is available, you can keep each person's .MMF file on it. If you choose this option, we recommend putting each .MMF file in a separate subdirectory, sharing the subdirectory across the network, and limiting access to that shared subdirectory through a password.

On the positive side, this solution puts the .MMF files in a convenient place where each user has good access. On the negative side, people will probably be less likely to clean out their old messages stored in their .MMF files if they have a lot of storage room on the mail server. Importantly, the time needed to access files on the network can increase under this arrangement because the Mail program must pull all the messages across the network each time it is used—significantly increasing network overhead and creating bottlenecks.

Generally, we recommend placing the .MMF on each person's desktop PC hard drive because that strategy minimizes network traffic. However, you don't have to use the same solution for every person on the network. Some people might be better off with .MMF files stored on the PC that acts as a Postoffice, and others might find it more efficient to keep the files on their local drives.

■ Specifying Notification of Messages

You can run the Mail program in two different ways: You can start it at the beginning of every day and leave it running, even as a minimized icon, or you can open and close it several times a day to see your mail. If you are very limited on processing power and RAM, then you should open and exit the program each time you use it. But most people will want to leave the program running—if only to get notification of incoming messages.

If you pull down the Mail menu in the Mail program, you'll see a choice called Options. This choice leads you to a menu where you can elect to have the program notify you of newly arriving mail by making a sound through your PC's speaker, by flashing the icon of an envelope on the screen, or both.

■ Making Mail

The Mail program in Windows for Workgroups takes full advantage of the graphical user interface—that's a fancy way of saying that you'll make heavy use of a mouse to create, read, store, and move mail. The interface is assisted by several icons on the Toolbar that, unlike the new icons on the Windows for Workgroups File Manager, carry clear labels designating their purpose. Figure 5.5 shows the Toolbar and menu bar in the Mail program.

Figure 5.5

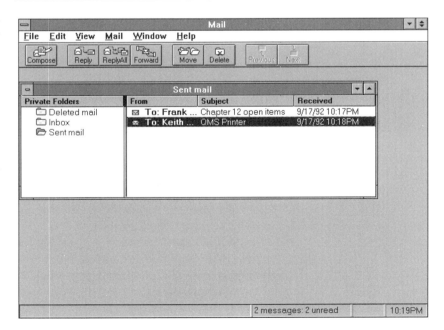

The icons on the Toolbar in the Mail program carry labels that clearly define their functions. You can quickly create and read messages using the icons. The pull-down menus have a few special functions, such as management of the mail system and cutting and pasting text, that don't appear as Toolbar icons.

Selecting the Compose icon starts off the process of creating a message. After the user selects Compose, the Send Note menu appears, as shown in Figure 5.6. The best course of action at this point is always to select the Address button. Our experience shows that people who try to enter user names from the keyboard often get the names wrong, so it is best to choose the names from the Address Book.

Figure 5.6

The Send Note menu appears after you click on the Compose icon on the Toolbar or select Compose Note from the Mail menu in the main Mail window.

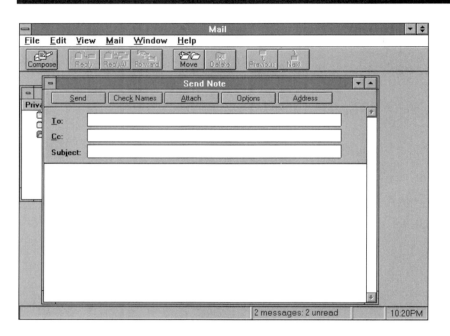

Addressing a Message

The Address Book, shown in Figure 5.7, is an extremely useful part of the electronic-mail system, and many people will want to take some time to personalize their Address Book lists. The default list of names that appears is the Postoffice List drawn from all account names registered in the Postoffice. However, these lists can often get too long for easy access and individuals might want to create a Personal Address Book of names.

You can create your own Personal Address Book by dragging and dropping names from the Postoffice list to the card file icon located next to the To and Cc buttons in the center of the screen. After you have the Personal Address Book loaded with all the appropriate names, you can switch to it by selecting the card file icon on the left side of the screen. Selecting the open book icon on the top left of the screen gives you options for moving back to the Postoffice list or selecting other address books.

Figure 5.7

The Address Book contains the full user names, not short aliases, of people with authorized mail accounts. These accounts might have been set up during the initial use of the mail software on each PC or by the administrator using the Postoffice Manager function in the Mail menu of the Mail window.

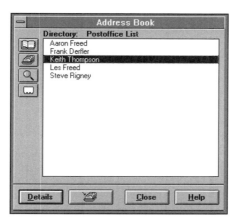

When you select the names of addressees from the lists in the Address Book, you typically select a name and then move to the To or Cc button to enter your choice. However, if you have several names you want in either field, the process of selecting and moving becomes tedious. As in all Windows programs, you can make multiple selections by holding down the Ctrl key on the keyboard while you use the mouse to click on each desired name. As Figure 5.8 shows, each name stays selected, and when you select To or Cc you move the entire list of names into the desired field. After you have the message completely addressed, click on OK at the bottom of the screen to move to the next step in preparing a message.

It often happens that while you are creating a message you find you need to add or delete an addressee. You can move back to the Address Book at any time without losing your work by clicking on the Address button on the menu. The program gives you excellent flexibility as you select, add, and delete addressees.

After you have the correct names in the To and Cc fields, you can move on to the Subject field and enter a descriptive subject for your text. Pausing a second to create a good descriptive subject line will make your message easier to find and reread for both you and your addressees. You can enter long subject names with more than 48 characters, but because only the first 23 characters appear in the Inbox window, they are the most important. The fastest way to move between the fields in the beginning of the message is to use the Tab key on the keyboard. You can also reposition the cursor with the mouse. Few people find using the Tab key to move between fields intuitive, but it is a standard Windows convention.

Figure 5.8

You can select multiple names from the list by holding down the Ctrl key on the keyboard and making selections with the left mouse button.

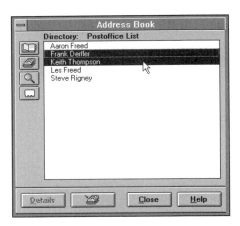

Mailing from the File Manager

Although you'll probably keep the Mail program running as a Windows application, sometimes you will be in other Windows applications, such as the File Manager, and want to send a file to someone on the network as a piece of mail. Windows for Workgroups has a Send Mail icon in the File Manager Toolbar. You can add the Send Mail button to other Toolbars by choosing the Options pull-down menu and selecting Customize Toolbar. You'll find the Send Mail button among the alternatives. Drag it onto the Toolbar using the left mouse button and drop it there.

If you don't see the Send Mail button in the list of alternatives, then use the File Manager to find WINFILE.INI in the WINDOWS\SYSTEM subdirectory. Double-click on the file to start the Notepad program. Move the cursor below the section called [Settings] and create a new section called [Addons]. Under that heading, add the following statement:

```
Send mail = C:\Windows\system\sendfile.dll
```

Then hit the Alt key to bring up the Edit menu, save the file, and exit the program. When you restart the File Manager, the Send Mail button should appear on the Toolbar.

After you initiate the Send Mail sequence from the File Manager or any other screen, you create and send your mail the same way you do from the Mail program.

Preparing the Text

The Windows environment makes it very easy to prepare text. The Mail program includes a word processor, shown in Figure 5.9, with line wrap at the 63d character of text and full editing features activated by the mouse. Selections from the pull-down menu allow you to cut, copy, and paste highlighted text. You can't drag and drop highlighted text like you can with many modern Windows word processors, but that is about the only ability you are ever likely to miss in the Mail text processor. Under the File option, the menu bar also provides menu choices for importing both ASCII text and graphical objects from other files on any drive.

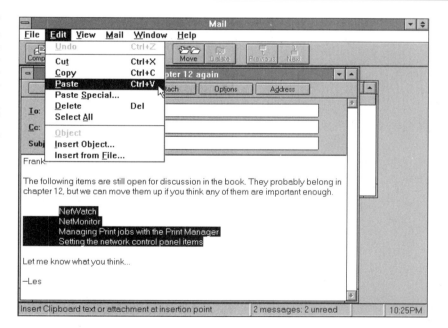

Figure 5.9

You have a wide range of text editing tools in the Mail program. There are Cut, Copy, and Paste options on the Edit pull-down menu. The File pull-down menu contains functions for importing text and graphical objects from files on any available disk drive.

However, there are some types of files, particularly binary program files or files in a specific spreadsheet or database format, that you don't want to insert into your message because they'll appear as gibberish on the screen. You can attach these files in their original format and use the electronic-mail system to move them to the addressee by clicking on the Attach button in the Send Note window.

This action will prompt you for a file name and provide a file-search menu, shown in Figure 5.10. You can move to other drives and select specific file extensions to make it easier to find the file(s) you want to attach.

76 Chapter 5: Using the Electronic Mail

Figure 5.10

When you need to attach a program or data file to a mail message, the menu helps you find the needed file. You can narrow the search by choosing only files with specific extensions for display in the window.

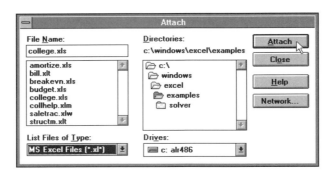

Putting Pictures in the Text

So far, we've described efficient but boring text messages. It's often true that you can get an idea across faster and more clearly with a drawing, diagram, chart, or picture or by using special fonts and characters. The mail system in Windows for Workgroups provides an excellent way to insert graphical objects from various types of programs into your mail messages. When the recipient reads the incoming mail, the photo or diagram appears in the message, as Figure 5.11 shows. This capability can help you create impressive messages with punch.

To create a message with a graphical object, you start in the normal manner. After you address the message, add a subject, and enter the introductory text, position the cursor where you want to place the graphical object. Then choose Insert Object from the Edit menu in the Mail window.

After this selection, a menu appears, showing applications in your PC capable of creating an object file. If you select an application such as Paintbrush, it opens over the Mail program. At this point you can open a file or create a diagram. When you are satisfied with the image, pull down the File menu in the Paintbrush program and choose Update. After you update the file, choose Return to Mail from the same pull-down menu and you'll return to the Mail program to find the object in the mail message.

Sometimes the image the addressee sees isn't the same as the one the originator prepared. Differences in video adapters and display systems in different machines generate differences in the images. Microsoft attempts to account for the differences, but an image might have a different color or lose detail if it is created on a machine with a high-density color graphics adapter and displayed on a machine with a less capable adapter.

Managing the Incoming Mail 77

Figure 5.11

A drawing can simply dress up your message or it can convey the meaning of the message. It isn't difficult to place a graphic object into a mail message, and the technique can help you to create impressive messages. Often, you can use the special fonts available in drawing programs to good effect.

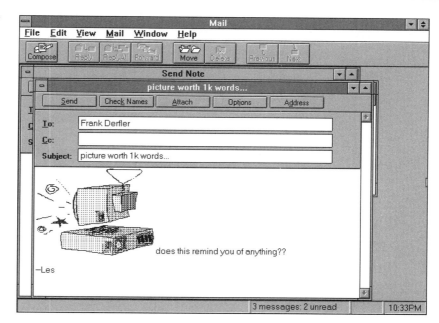

Although we've referred to the objects you can insert in a message as pictures or drawings, you can also insert sounds from programs that can create sound files in the appropriate format. Of course, the receiving system must have the proper equipment to create the sound received in the mail message.

Sending It Off

After the preparation of the text, sending the message is simple. You select the Send button from the Toolbar, and the message moves into an outgoing queue. The queue will be emptied when the program next checks with the Postoffice at a scheduled time or when you choose the Exit or Exit and Sign Out option from the File pull-down menu in the Mail menu bar. If you have mail waiting to go out, you should allow Mail to send the messages before exiting.

■ Managing the Incoming Mail

Reading incoming mail is easy. You simply double-click on the Inbox icon or on the Private Folders icon in the Mail window to activate the Inbox window shown in Figure 5.12.

Figure 5.12

The Inbox Window displays newly arrived messages and messages you have read but not disposed of.

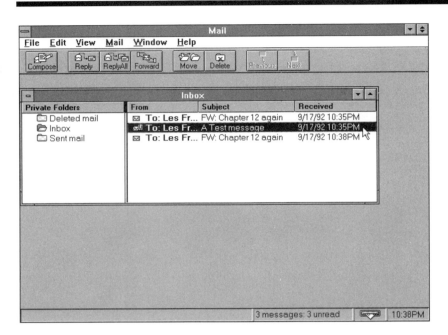

The Inbox button bar includes buttons you can select with the mouse to generate a reply to the originator of a message, to reply to all addressees, to forward a message to other addressees, to move a message to one of the special folders, and to delete a message.

The task of formulating a reply to a message is made easier because the Windows for Workgroups Mail program opens the reply window just above the text of the incoming message. In this way, you can easily see the items you want to reply to or comment on. If you want to include segments of the original message in the reply, you'll have to use the Copy and Paste commands to move them into the reply field. Forwarding is an important option because it allows you to move a message requiring action to the appropriate persons for that action. When you forward a message, you can add your own comments.

The Inbox screen has four buttons: Private Folders, From, Subject, and Received. The last three options sort the messages in the Inbox according to the button you select with the mouse. Each button initiates a re-sort of the messages by a different priority.

The left side of the Inbox window, Private Folders, opens many more options. The standard folders in the left segment are Deleted Mail, Inbox, and Sent Mail. These folders represent a primitive way you can segment and archive your messages, but you'll probably want to add folders on more

Managing the Incoming Mail 79

specific subjects to the basic set. After you add special subject folders, you can drag and drop messages from the Inbox into any of the private folders.

You start the process of creating new folders customized for your needs by selecting the Move button from the File button bar. Selecting this option brings up the Move Message window shown in Figure 5.13. Selecting the New button on the right side of the window allows you to create new folders. You'll find yourself creating folders for special projects and for discussions of ongoing issues. One of the most interesting options, available through the Options button, allows you to create new folders under existing folders, so that you can keep track of messages from specific people or messages on a related subtopic. The folder system is the key to keeping track of important messages and to deleting messages to recover disk space once the messages have outlived their usefulness.

Figure 5.13

The Move Message window contains important options that will help you track and find messages. In this figure, the New button has been selected and options for new folders are shown.

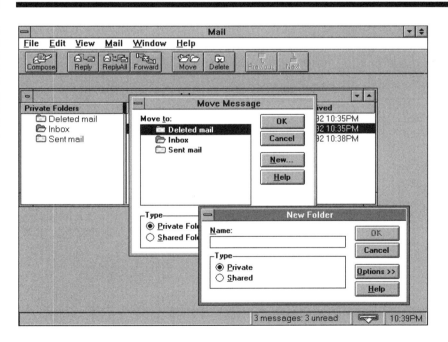

Sharing Folders

At the bottom of the Move Message window you'll see an option for making private folders or shared folders. Shared folders are the closest thing to special-subject bulletin boards you'll find in this version of Microsoft Mail. When you create a new shared folder, you can specify the rights you want to give to other users. The default rights for new shared folders are Read and Write. Under this setup, anyone on the network can place messages, including messages with inserted objects or even attached binary files, in a message folder labeled for a specific subject. People who are interested in that subject or who need to know the information in the shared folder can select it and page through it at any time. This sharing technique can reduce the number of "Cc:" addressees on messages and reduce overall network traffic. You can also give users the ability to delete material from the shared folder, although you typically wouldn't set the system up in that way.

Shared folders provide a common place to post messages about items for sale or carpool rides, but they are also a valuable tool for people working on projects in workgroups. For example, you can leave the text of a detailed analysis for peer review and comment. Any group project can have its own shared folders. They improve productivity and facilitate interaction by keeping everything in one place.

Finding Messages

In all the folders, including the Inbox, you can use the sorting tools to sort messages alphabetically by subject, alphabetically by sender, or according to the time and date received. If you want to sort messages in reverse order, hold down the Ctrl key while you click on the desired sorting button.

You can also set up the Mail program to sort important messages using the Message Finder. Pull down the File menu in the Mail window and select the Message Finder option. Then type in your sorting criteria. For example, you might want to automatically identify all messages from your boss. Type the name of your boss in the From field and then choose the Start button. You can minimize the Message Finder and it will continue to search and sort your messages as they arrive.

■ Managing the Mail System

There are two important things to remember about management of the Windows for Workgroups Mail system. First, only the user who created the Postoffice shared directory can manage the Postoffice, so it is very wise to make sure that a higher-level manager knows that user's password. We strongly suggest that you create a network user named Admin and then use the Admin account to create the Postoffice.

Second, the manager doesn't have a lot of software tools in this system. Much of the responsibility for deleting old messages falls on the individuals. Because individuals usually like to store messages indefinitely, the manager of the mail system might have to apply administrative pressure to convince users to clean out old folders.

The Mail pull-down menu contains a selection called Postoffice Manager. (This option only appears when you are logged in under the same user name that created the Postoffice.) This selection moves you to the Postoffice Manager screen, shown in Figure 5.14. From this screen you can add and remove users and manage the shared file folders. Typically, you'll add users when more than one person is sharing a PC and the Mail program has already run through its initial setup sequence.

Figure 5.14

The Postoffice Manager menu allows you to add and delete user names and aliases. Only the user who created the Postoffice can access this menu.

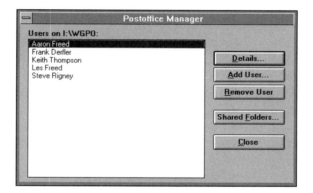

The Postoffice Manager option also allows you to compress the shared folders so they take up less disk space. However, even the Postoffice Manager can be prevented from removing shared folders if the shared folder was not originally created with that option.

The Windows for Workgroups Mail program is an engine for creation and coordination. As we'll see in the following chapter, the program provides a platform for a number of exciting and practical applications that propel the work flow of a group.

- *Forms Handling*
- *Schedule+ Basics*
- *A Few Tips*

CHAPTER

The First Forms Program: Schedule+

IN MANY ORGANIZATIONS, SCHEDULING THREE OR MORE BUSY people for a meeting, along with arranging for a conference room and slide projector, can be a frustrating and time-consuming task requiring several phone calls. If one person or facility isn't available at the time the other people or facilities are, a series of negotiations begins. Mathematicians refer to this method of simultaneously handling several unknown factors as progressive approximation, but whoever must make all the contacts and coordinate the compromises will call it frustration. Before you finally resolve the scheduling problem, the number of phone calls you'll make to schedule a meeting can grow exponentially.

LAN scheduling products such as Schedule+ simplify this task and often completely remove the frustration. If everyone in the organization uses the scheduling software, one person can access the public calendars of other people and resources to quickly find out when there is common free time. The process doesn't involve any invasion of privacy; the meeting planner doesn't see every detail on a personal calendar, just enough to find the free time.

The Schedule+ program bundled with Windows for Workgroups is the first of what will certainly be a series of mail-enabled applications from Microsoft and other companies. This program uses the electronic-mail engine to find the names of people using the network and to move notifications and acknowledgments of appointments across the network. The scheduling system won't work without a properly installed and operational mail system. Before we delve into how to use Schedule+, let's look at the concept of forms handling and see the impact it will have on networked software and workgroups.

■ Forms Handling

The concept of forms is fundamental to Microsoft's vision of workgroup productivity. The term *forms* in this context is very broad and touches every aspect of the interaction of people in business, government, and academic workgroups.

Businesses and workgroups larger than just a few people run on forms. Some forms, such as mail-routing slips, remain as paper throughout their useful life. But other forms, such as credit applications, are typically just the first step toward entry into a computer database. Many forms, such as receipts or invoices, are the paper output of computer systems. The concept that the people at Microsoft are using is simple: Automate the forms—all forms—so they never become paper. Then route the forms electronically, often along multiple paths simultaneously, to manage and speed the group process.

Schedule+ is a simple forms application. Each person's calendar is a form with entries for the date, the time, and annotations. Programs running on each PC can gather the forms, compare the entries, and look for scheduling conflicts or for opportunities to schedule an appointment—in effect to make another mark on the form.

In the next level of complexity, evolving programs will enable people in a workgroup to design specific forms to fit the special functions of the group. New programs will automatically route forms, based on the entries in certain fields of the forms, between certain people. Users will learn to set reminders and tickler messages to keep the process efficient and use the lookup and search capabilities in the programs to find information and alternatives for entry into the forms.

The forms analogy can extend to retrieving information from shared databases with complex indexes. Today, when you enter or retrieve data in a database, you typically use an on-screen form that is part of a specific application. But consider a system of standardized yet customized on-screen forms containing (or able to obtain) information on how to route themselves to an appropriate shared database—like a great shared filing cabinet. Microsoft is working on a shared workgroup memory system similar in concept to the information-sharing product called Lotus Notes. Microsoft's program developers can create a shared group memory that relies not on one specific application, but rather on the common basis of forms and the electronic-mail-forms transport engine.

The ubiquitous networking and electronic-mail services provided by Windows for Workgroups create a firm basis for a forms-processing system. It is relatively simple to write forms applications, so you'll be able to choose from plenty of alternative products for your business or create your own forms system in-house. The key to deciding which form product to buy for a particular type of business or application will be the product's ability to interoperate with other similar products riding over the electronic mail "forms engine." The era of stand-alone applications for personal computers and workgroups is over. Applications must work together to help the workgroup process, so don't buy a workgroup productivity application that doesn't interoperate.

■ Schedule+ Basics

Even the best scheduling software is useless if users don't cooperate by keeping their personal calendars current. Obviously, these personal calendars are at the heart of the group-scheduling process. Group scheduling often starts out as a top-down directed activity, but group peer pressure usually keeps it rolling so that individuals become accustomed to using their personal calendars.

People won't use calendars that aren't readily available or easy to use. DOS programs have to use memory-robbing terminate-and-stay-resident programs (TSRs) to keep the electronic calendar handy. Fortunately, the multitasking Windows environment makes it easy to keep the calendar program running so you can pop between different applications and come back to your calendar when you need it. Because Schedule+ runs over the electronic-mail program, notifications of schedule changes come as e-mail messages announced by a chime and/or a flashing mail icon.

Schedule+ is only one of, approximately, a dozen scheduling programs on the market, but all these programs provide a common set of features. Although Microsoft bundles Schedule+ into Windows for Workgroups, Schedule+ isn't a give-away program with a skeletal set of operations. It has a very competitive set of features and an excellent interface for the user; its major weakness is in handling shared resources such as meeting rooms. Here are the most important features of scheduling programs and the ways each feature is implemented in Windows for Workgroups.

Presentations and Views

Scheduling programs vary in how they present their scheduled events and free time. Some packages display graphs of conflicting and open schedule times. Others let you work from a graphical representation of calendar pages, and a few programs use text explanations to outline the scheduling options. The Schedule+ program in Windows for Workgroups provides a variety of views ranging from a bar graph that shows conflicting and open times to a calendar page with added space for notes. Figure 6.1 shows the main appointments calendar for Schedule+. By clicking on the tabs on the side of the screen, you can change to other views.

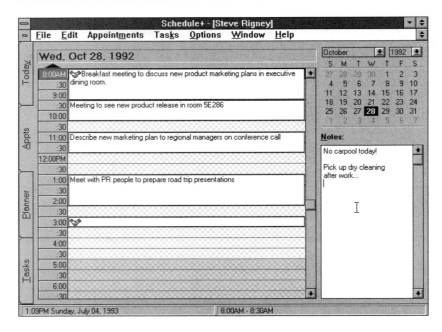

Figure 6.1

The appointments screen shows the duration of each appointment and allows you to describe its purpose. You can easily switch to other views, including a planning graph that lets you show the busy and free times of other people in the workgroup, by clicking on the tabs on the left side of the screen.

Invitations and Confirmations

Scheduling programs also vary in how they confirm the proposed events. The simpler packages assume that if the event fits on the calendar, the people scheduled to attend will be there. Because it runs on top of the electronic-mail program, Schedule+ provides an efficient series of meeting notification and acknowledgment messages. The requests and acknowledgments have automated functions, which allow you to confirm attendance at a meeting without typing a word—part of the concept of forms handling—but they also allow you to personalize the replies. Figure 6.2 shows a meeting notification message and the options for a reply. You see these messages by selecting the Messages option from the Windows pull-down menu.

Figure 6.2

The meeting request is a simple electronic-mail message containing notification of a tentative meeting and a request for a reply. It is easy to reply by selecting the Accept, Decline, or Tentative button. That mouse action is the only action you need to take. You can include text in your reply or view your schedule to check for conflicts.

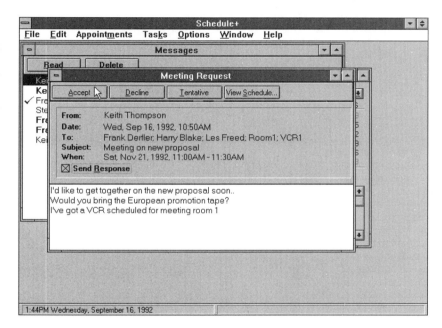

User Names

Schedule+ gets its base of user names from the electronic-mail program in Windows for Workgroups, so you don't have to set it up as a separate application. When you double-click on the Schedule+ icon (), it is ready to run. As we described in the last chapter, the electronic-mail system automatically attempts to enroll new users, but the administrator of the Postoffice still must manually enter anyone sharing a PC.

Scheduling of Shared Resources

One problem common to the programs in this class is that they don't provide an easy way to schedule a pool of shared resources, such as a group of conference rooms. Since a group of resources—for example, three conference rooms or three slide projectors—usually has only one manager, it's wasteful to make that manager repeatedly check each separate account for each shared room or device to confirm its status. The person scheduling the meeting and the person managing the resources should not have to treat each identical projector, VCR, viewing screen, or meeting room as a separate entity.

Unfortunately, Microsoft didn't provide a smooth way to handle shared resources. As Figure 6.3 illustrates, you must make a separate user identification—actually an electronic-mail alias described in Chapter 5—for each conference room, slide projector, or VCR that you want to use. Then you try to schedule each item on a hit-or-miss basis. You can schedule the use of these resources either by bringing them into the planning bar chart or by selecting the Open Other's Appt. Book option from the File pull-down menu in the Schedule+ main screen. Other competing programs allow you to put these common resources, like two identical VCRs, in a common pool.

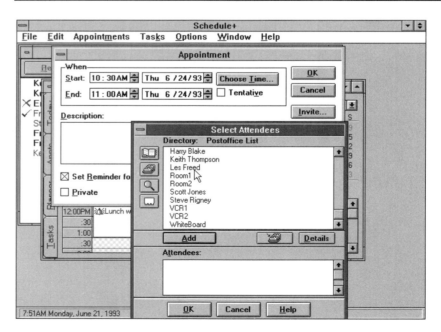

Figure 6.3

The person who created the Postoffice for the mail program has added user names for shared resources, such as Room1, Room2, VCR1, and VCR2, to the list of users. These names appear as potential meeting attendees in the Schedule+ menu. You can schedule the use of these resources either by bringing them into the planning bar chart or by opening the appointment book for each resource.

Distribution Lists

You often have a group of people who are interested in knowing about every meeting on a specific topic. The mail program in Windows for Workgroups makes it easy to create specific groups of addressees that you can invite to every meeting using Schedule+. As described in Chapter 5, you can create a Personal Address Book of people interested in specific topics.

Holidays

The company calendar is important to everyone—if only to know which days are holidays. Under Schedule+ you can import a central company calendar into any user's calendar and see the company holidays and special events. As demonstrated in Figure 6.4, the electronic-mail administrator should create a user called Company so that someone can enter a calendar under this name, and so that others can find the calendar and import it. It's important to give all others the ability to read this calendar.

Figure 6.4

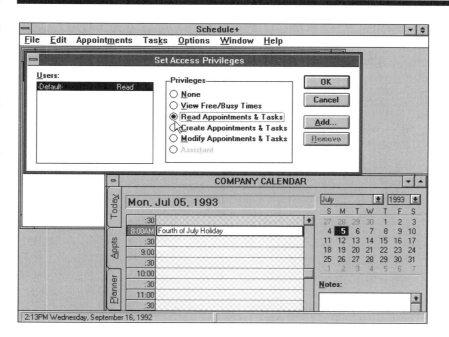

The administrator of the Postoffice has created a user called Company and entered all of the company holidays and events into the calendar for this user. The Set Access Privileges selection under the Options pull-down menu brings up a set of privileges available to all network users. Allowing everyone to read the company calendar makes it easy to import its contents into personal calendars.

Tasks

Some things that you want to schedule aren't specific appointments, but fall into the category of tasks you must perform—often as part of a bigger project. Schedule+ allows you to set up tasks on specific dates or on a recurring basis. The task manager in Schedule+ is really the beginning of a project-management system. You can set due dates for tasks, set priorities, and record when a task is completed. The system doesn't generate the graphs and projections that are part of robust project-management programs, but Schedule+ is quite adequate for many projects—particularly those that don't involve managing a budget or an inventory of materials.

Figure 6.5 illustrates one individual's tasks that are part of a larger project. Selecting the Add to Schedule button on the bottom of the window places the tasks on the daily appointment calendars. A project manager who has the rights to create appointments and tasks, as described later in the chapter, could enter these tasks into an individual's task list.

Figure 6.5

You get to the Tasks screen by clicking on the tab labeled Tasks on the left side of the window, not by choosing the Tasks pull-down menu. These four tasks for one individual are part of a larger project for the workgroup. You can set different priorities for the tasks and sort them by project, due date, or task description.

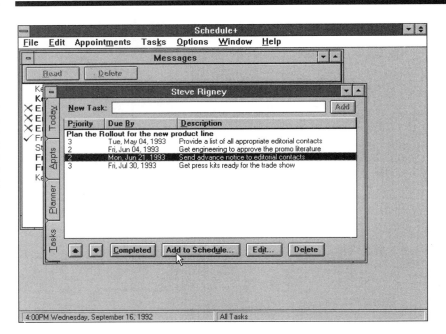

Notes and To-Do Lists

Calendars are handy places for jotting down notes to yourself or for creating a list of things to do. The Schedule+ appointments calendar provides a Notes area for every calendar day. You have full editing capabilities in this section, including the Copy and Paste commands, which make it easy to move and copy information between days.

Meeting Times

Automated systems can make comparisons quickly. The Auto-Pick command on the Appointments menu in Schedule+ Planner can quickly compare the schedules of a large number of people and resources and find the amount of common free time specified. As shown in Figure 6.6, Auto-Pick works smoothly, displaying the prospective meeting times on a bar chart. If you select Auto-Pick again, it finds the next alternative in the time sequence. This ability to look again is particularly handy when the Auto-Pick function spots, for example, a time late on Friday afternoon—a time that's free but not ideal for settling down to a meeting.

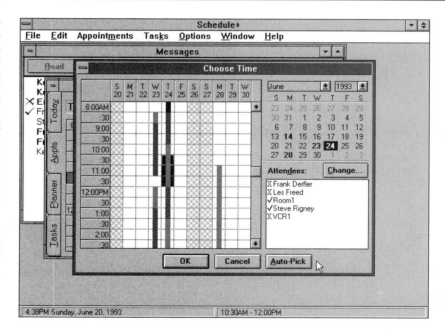

Figure 6.6

This bar graph shows an attempt to bring three people together in a meeting room equipped with a VCR. The check marks in front of the names in the lower-right corner indicate that one person and a meeting room are free at the time the user proposed: from 10:30 to 11:30 on June 24. The *X* indicates that two people and the VCR are busy. The crosshatched lines on the bar graph also represent scheduling conflicts. It looks as if parts of Wednesday and all day Friday are available. Selecting the Auto-Pick will tell the program to find the next available spot for the meeting.

Access rights

Privacy is important, so typically you'll limit the access other people have to your calendar so they see only that you are busy, and not why you are busy. However, there might be times, perhaps in a smaller office, when it is useful to allow more intimate access. Schedule+ allows you to protect your calendar with five general levels of access privileges that you can assign to all users or just to certain people. The program also provides for a special-access arrangement called Assistant that allows a specified person to send and receive messages on your behalf. See the last section in this chapter for more specific information on setting up access-privilege levels.

Recurring Events

If you have a regular meeting the second Tuesday of every month, it would be handy to enter this meeting only once and let the software insert it into the correct dates. The Appointments pull-down menu includes options that allow you to set and edit recurring appointments. After selecting the New Recurring Appointments option from the Appointments menu, you can access the two menus shown in Figure 6.7. The Recurring Appointment menu allows you to quickly set a recurring appointment using a weekly meeting as a default. If you click on the Change button, you can use the Change Recurrence menu to set the meeting to monthly, biweekly, or other time intervals.

Figure 6.7

The Recurring Appointment menu provides a way to quickly enter an appointment that comes up on a regular basis. You set the time and interval once, and the program enters the appointment into your calendar for a year or forever, depending on the option you set in the Change Recurrence menu.

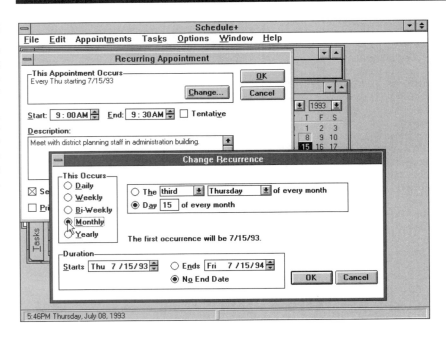

Printed Calendars

Notebook and laptop computers are great, but they still aren't quite as portable as a piece of paper. Every useful scheduling program should have the ability to produce a printout. The Schedule+ windows shown in Figure 6.8 can help you print a variety of page arrangements and views. You initiate printing by selecting the Print option from the File pull-down menu.

Figure 6.8

The Print and Print Setup dialog boxes offer a variety of ways to print out the various calendar and planning dialog boxes in Schedule+. You can choose the daily view (a calendar page with notes), the bar chart from the planner view, or a list of tasks. The landscape orientation works well for printing all these views.

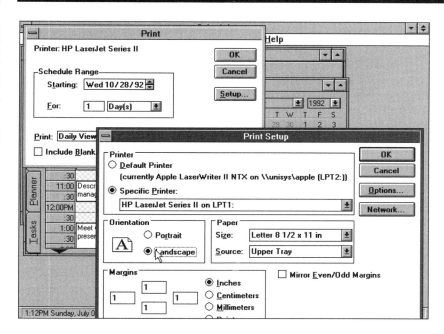

Searches

If you're looking for a meeting scheduled weeks in the future or for something you did months in the past, it's useful to have a way to search for key words and events. To help, Schedule+ has a Find option under the Edit pull-down menu in the Schedule+ window. Selecting this option, shown in Figure 6.9, starts a convenient utility that can search for a single word in the title or text of a meeting or task.

■ A Few Tips

Because of its many self-explanatory menus and buttons, Schedule+ is very easy to use. But here are a few tips we developed while using the program in our workgroup.

Figure 6.9

We used the Find selection in the Edit pull-down menu to look for the word *study* in the appointment calendar. The program found the study group appointment and displayed it. The Find utility, which isn't sensitive to the capitalization of the letters, will look for words within the text of an appointment note.

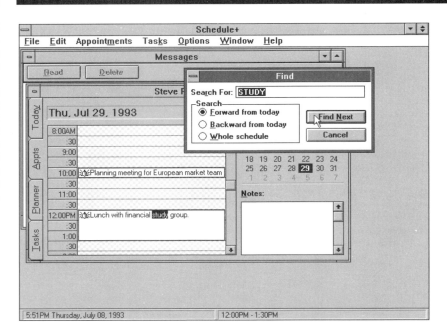

Set the Meeting with the Mouse

You can highlight the time for a meeting by holding the left mouse button down and dragging the cursor across the time slots you want to select before clicking on the New Appointment option from the Appointments pull-down menu. In Figure 6.10, we used the cursor to select the time from 9:00 to 10:30 a.m. The selected time span appears in the windows of the Appointment dialog box, shown in Figure 6.11. It is much easier to use the cursor to set the time than it is to click on the spin buttons in the dialog box.

Drag and Drop Tasks

The task-management capabilities of Schedule+ have been unheralded. These capabilities are easy to use, yet powerful enough to manage major group projects. In Figure 6.12, we show two major projects with a short series of tasks under each one. Since some tasks might be common or reused in both projects, you can drag and drop a task from one project to the other. You can select only one task at a time. In Figure 6.13, the task "Provide a list of editorial contacts" has moved into the top project list.

A Few Tips **95**

Figure 6.10

We held down the left mouse button and dragged the cursor across the time slots for the meeting.

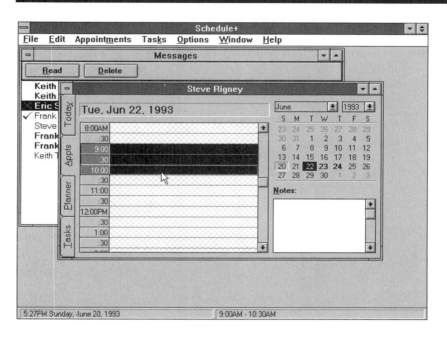

Figure 6.11

The time we indicated in Figure 6.9 shows up in the Appointment dialog box. If you use this technique, you're ready to enter the appointment information and quickly move on to other tasks.

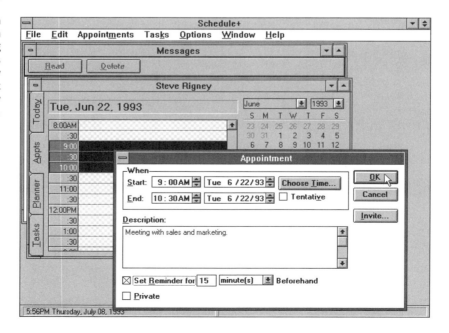

96   Chapter 6: The First Forms Program: Schedule+

Figure 6.12

This window shows two major projects with several tasks under each project.

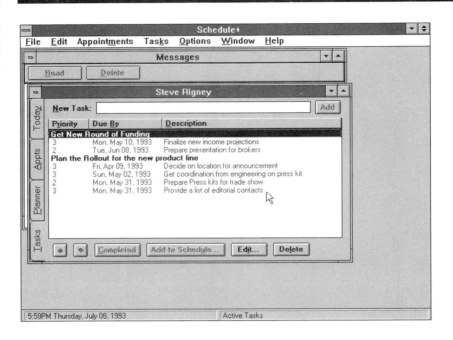

Figure 6.13

We used a drag-and-drop technique to move the task "Provide a list of editorial contacts" from one project to the other. The ability to drag and drop a line of text is, typically, part of powerful and modern word processing programs, but it works well in this scheduling program too.

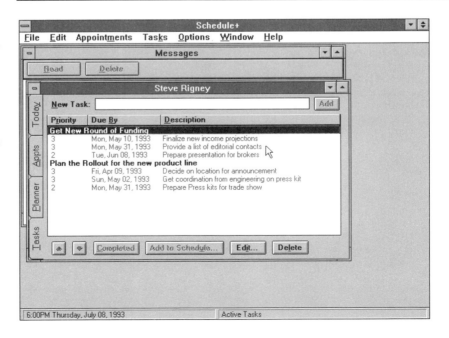

Click on the Busy Bar

Figure 6.14 shows an attempt by a user named Steve to set up a meeting with two other people in Conference Room 1 on Wednesday. The bars on the calendar and the check marks in the box in the lower-right corner inform Steve that he is the only one with a conflict. If Steve double-clicks on the bar in the chart, the display will move to his planning calendar so he can see the specific appointment and make a decision about which meeting should take precedence.

Figure 6.14

The squares displayed on Wednesday the 23 indicate the desired block of time for a meeting. The solid bar indicates a previous appointment. The crosshatched bars show that other potential attendees also have scheduled appointments in those time blocks. Different degrees of cross-hatching show different degrees of conflict. Double-clicking on the solid bar brings up the appointment calendar for that date and time.

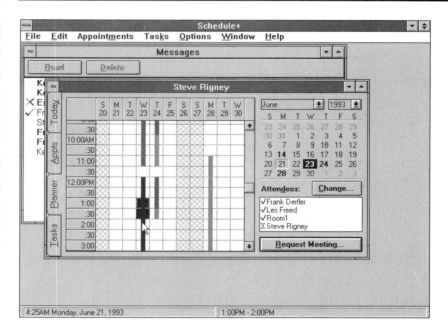

Set Access Privileges

The process for setting access privileges isn't clear from the menu. You arrive at the screen shown in Figure 6.15 by selecting Set Access Privileges from the Options pull-down menu. When the Set Access Privileges dialog box first appears, the only user name in the left box is Default. If you want to give other privileges to specific people or to deny someone access to your schedule, click on the Add button to bring up the Add Users window. You can't use this window to add new users into the Schedule+ system; that is done through the Postoffice mail system. This screen allows you to add users to your access privilege list.

Chapter 6: The First Forms Program: Schedule+

Figure 6.15

Granting access rights is a powerful feature of the Schedule+ program. Your options range from denying anyone the right to obtain any information about your calendar to allowing someone to have full use of your calendar.

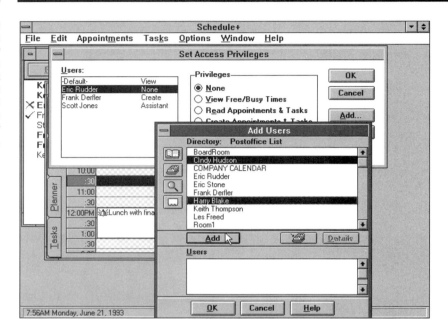

You select a name from the list of users by clicking on it and then clicking on the Add button. You can select more than one name by holding down the Ctrl key while you make the selections with the mouse. After you select Add, the names move down into the Users box. At that point, you must select OK to move the names into the Users box in the Set Access Privileges dialog box. Then, you must select each name in the Users box and give it an associated privilege by making a selection from the Privileges box. A lot of actions are needed to add people to your access list with the proper level of access rights, and since this isn't something you do often, the process can become confusing.

- *Who Needs a Server, Anyway?*
- *Using NetWare with Windows for Workgroups*
- *Using LAN Manager with Windows for Workgroups*
- *Sharing Files and Printers with Macintosh Computers*

CHAPTER

7

Using Windows for Workgroups with Other Networks

So far, we've examined Windows for Workgroups in its role as stand-alone peer-to-peer network. In this chapter, we'll show you how to use Windows for Workgroups in conjunction with Microsoft's LAN Manager and Novell's NetWare. LAN Manager and NetWare both support Macintosh clients, so we'll also show you how to share files with Mac users via these two networks.

■ Who Needs a Server, Anyway?

At first glance, Windows for Workgroups appears to target the elusive "low" end of the network marketplace. Peer-to-peer networks, no matter how good or powerful, are invariably categorized as low-end networks. There are a couple of valid reasons for this typecasting, but Windows for Workgroups breaks the mold by providing excellent integration with server-based networks.

Peer-to-peer networks such as LANtastic, 10NET, and NetWare Lite provide file- and printer-sharing services much like those in Windows for Workgroups. All three have won critical acclaim for performance and flexibility—within their limits. Virtually all peer-to-peer networks (including Windows for Workgroups) are based on MS-DOS. Although DOS is a serviceable operating system for stand-alone PCs, it wasn't designed to provide the kind of real-time multitasking services that heavy-duty network operating systems require. In addition, the DOS file structure was designed for a single-user system; network file servers are inherently multiuser machines. Microsoft's LAN Manager runs under OS/2, and a forthcoming version will run under Windows/NT. While OS/2 hasn't become popular as a desktop operating system (please, no letters from IBM OS/2 2.0 devotees!), it does provide efficient multitasking. OS/2 and Windows/NT use Microsoft's High Performance File System (HPFS), which provides a more efficient directory structure, support for long file names, and higher performance than DOS. The result is that a LAN Manager server is faster than a Windows for Workgroups server, especially when serving more than one client.

Novell's NetWare doesn't run under DOS either. Because no viable multiuser PC operating system existed when NetWare was introduced back in 1983, Novell's engineers followed a time-honored tradition among software engineers: They wrote their own operating system. A server running NetWare is literally running NetWare. A NetWare server boots NetWare just like a DOS machine boots DOS. Like OS/2, NetWare can easily handle file and printer requests from several users at once. And like OS/2's HPFS, NetWare servers use a non-DOS disk format. Files on a NetWare server look like DOS files, but they reside on the server's disk in Novell's own proprietary format. The Novell disk format provides lightning-fast disk access, comprehensive access security, and support for non-DOS operating systems such as Macintosh, OS/2, and Unix. Novell also has the benefit of experience—NetWare has been around in one form or another for ten years.

In addition to their performance edge, server-based networks have other advantages that make them the tool of choice for large networks:

Security LAN Manager and NetWare provide comprehensive security features that allow the system administrator to precisely control each user's access to the network. Windows for Workgroups uses a simple but effective password system to protect confidential data.

Reliability NetWare offers reliability features such as disk mirroring and disk duplexing. These disk management schemes store data on multiple hard drives to provide an immediate, on-line backup and protection against catastrophic disk failures. Because Windows for Workgroups is based on DOS, it can't provide these advanced reliability features.

Centralized Administration NetWare and LAN Manager allow network supervisors to maintain a master list of user names, passwords, and file rights. By contrast, Windows for Workgroups maintains a separate password list on each networked PC, making administration much more difficult.

Additional Services LAN Manager and NetWare can provide other features such as pooled modems, shared mainframe connections, and multiple-site LAN bridging. Windows for Workgroups provides just basic file and printer sharing.

Multiplatform Support LAN Manager and NetWare support client PCs and minicomputers running DOS, OS/2, Macintosh, and Unix. Windows for Workgroups client PCs must be running DOS or Windows.

For all their advantages, server-based networks aren't for everyone. They can be difficult to install and maintain and require a dedicated high-powered PC to act as the server. Both LAN Manager and NetWare are expensive and may be overkill for many small companies. Still, if you need more networking power than Windows for Workgroups can deliver, you'll need to turn to a server-based network.

Like most other peer-to-peer network systems, Windows for Workgroups runs on top of DOS. Unlike the other peer networks (with the exception of Artisoft's LANtastic for NetWare), Windows for Workgroups can easily integrate into an existing LAN Manager or NetWare network, or even to both at once. The Windows for Workgroups retail package includes everything you need to connect your Windows for Workgroups PC to LAN Manager and NetWare networks.

This built-in connectivity offers the flexibility of a peer network while still providing a direct connection to a higher-powered server-based network.

In the following sections, we'll show you how Windows for Workgroups, LAN Manager, and NetWare can all work together.

■ Using NetWare with Windows for Workgroups

Over the years, Novell has sold NetWare in several variations, including ELS NetWare, Advanced NetWare 286, SFT NetWare 286, and NetWare 386. The current NetWare product line consists of two basic products, named NetWare 2 and NetWare 3. For our purposes in this chapter, all the variants of NetWare operate essentially the same way. For more detailed information on NetWare, see *PC Magazine Guide to Using NetWare,* by Les Freed and Frank Derfler, also published by Ziff-Davis Press.

NetWare is a server-based system, meaning that the shared resources reside on a central computer called a server. An individual PC connected to a NetWare network is called a client workstation. NetWare file servers make files, printers, and specialized peripherals available to the client PCs on the network. NetWare allows more than one server to exist on a single network, and physically distant servers can be linked together via telephone lines. A typical NetWare network consists of one or more servers and up to several hundred clients.

A workstation is simply an ordinary PC equipped with the proper hardware and software to communicate with the server. It's important to understand that a NetWare network and a Windows for Workgroups network can share network adapters and cabling. You don't need to install any additional hardware or cabling to use both networks simultaneously.

The NetWare DOS Client Software

Novell provides two different client software packages for use with NetWare. The original NetWare client software uses two TSR programs named IPX.COM and NETX.COM to connect workstations to the network. The IPX.COM program is hardware specific; it must be custom-built to match your PC's combination of network board, address, and IRQ settings. This customization is usually done by the NetWare system administrator, using a program called WSGEN. The newer client software package is called the Open Data-Link Interface (ODI). The ODI package uses four TSR programs: LSL.COM, IPXODI.COM, a hardware-specific driver, and the same NETX.COM program used by the classic NetWare drivers. The ODI drivers are more flexible than the older drivers, but Windows for Workgroups does not work with the ODI drivers.

The Windows for Workgroups retail package includes the latest version of the classic NetWare workstation software, but requires that you have a correctly configured IPX.COM program available on your PC. If you're using the ODI drivers, you must obtain and configure the standard NetWare IPX driver for your network board before you can use NetWare with Windows for Workgroups.

Installing NetWare Support in Windows for Workgroups

If the NetWare shell program (NETX) is loaded when you run the Windows for Workgroups SETUP.EXE program, SETUP will automatically install the Windows NetWare drivers for you. If you didn't have NetWare loaded when you initially installed Windows for Workgroups, you can install the NetWare drivers from the Network module of the Windows Control Panel. To install the NetWare drivers, follow these steps:

1. Load IPX and NETX from the DOS command line.

2. Start Windows and open the Control Panel.

3. Double-click on the Network icon and the Network Settings dialog box appears on the screen.

4. Click on the Networks icon at the bottom of the dialog box.

5. Select Novell NetWare from the list of supported networks and click on the Add button.

6. When asked, insert the floppy containing the NetWare drivers.

As part of the NetWare installation process, Windows adds several commands to your CONFIG.SYS and AUTOEXEC.BAT files. These commands load IPX and NETX at boot time, thus ensuring that the NetWare workstation software will be loaded before Windows starts. Windows adds the following lines to CONFIG.SYS:

```
DEVICE=C:\WINDOWS\MSIPX.SYS
LASTDRIVE=P
```

And it adds the following lines to AUTOEXEC.BAT:

```
C:\WINDOWS\MSIPX
C:\WINDOWS\NETX
```

The DEVICE=C:\WINDOWS\MSIPX.SYS command in the CONFIG.SYS file loads a driver that allows one network card to support both NetWare's IPX protocol and Microsoft's NetBEUI protocol. The LASTDRIVE statement in CONFIG.SYS determines which logical drive letters are available for NetWare to use. With LASTDRIVE set to P:, Windows for Workgroups can use drives up to and including drive P:—the remaining drive letters will be reserved for NetWare.

The MSIPX and NETX commands in AUTOEXEC.BAT load a modified version of your IPX.COM and the NetWare NETX.COM workstation software. MSIPX.COM replaces your original IPX.COM protocol driver. Because these drivers are fully compatible with the original NetWare workstation software, you can still access your NetWare network from DOS.

Once you've completed the installation steps outlined above, you must exit Windows and restart your PC to load the new NetWare drivers. When you reboot your PC, your NetWare login drive will be one letter higher than the letter specified in LASTDRIVE, so it will usually be Q. Switch to your login drive and run the NetWare LOGIN program before you start Windows.

Fine-Tuning NetWare for Windows

Once you've installed and tested the Windows NetWare drivers, you may find that you need to change some of the NetWare driver options. Most of these options are accessible from the Network module of the Control Panel. To see the NetWare options screen, follow these steps:

1. Start Windows and open the Control Panel.
2. Double-click on the Network icon.
3. Click on the Networks icon to change the network settings.
4. Click on Novell NetWare, and then click on the Settings button to see the NetWare settings (Figure 7.1).

Figure 7.1

Specifying NetWare settings from the Control Panel.

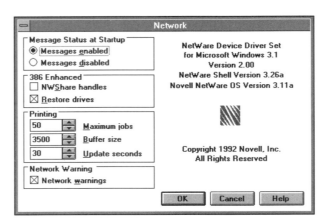

As you can see from Figure 7.1, the Control Panel settings for NetWare are separated into four groups: Message Status at Startup, 386 Enhanced, Printing, and Network Warning.

The first group, Message Status at Startup, determines whether your PC will receive NetWare broadcast messages. If you want to receive broadcast messages, select Messages Enabled. If you don't want to receive messages, select Messages Disabled.

The second group of settings, 386 Enhanced, determines how NetWare will handle network drive mappings when your PC is running Windows in 386-Enhanced mode. The NWShare handles setting is a simple check box, but requires a lengthy explanation.

When you run Windows on a stand-alone PC, Windows can be sure that the disk drives aren't going to change. If you have drives A: and C:, Windows knows that those are a hard-disk drive and a floppy drive and that they aren't going to go away while Windows is running. On a network, Windows cannot make this assumption because NetWare allows you to add, delete, and change drive mappings at any time. On a 386 system, Windows allows you to have several "virtual machines," each running a separate DOS program.

This flexibility can cause some problems. If you have a DOS program running in a window, and that program is using a data file on drive F:, what will happen if you go to the File Manager and disconnect drive F:? The answer depends on the NWShare Handles setting.

When NWShare Handles is disabled, Windows uses a drive mapping technique called Inherited Resource Visibility. This means that any new program you start inherits the drive and printer mappings that are already in place. If you change the drive or printer mappings from one program, any other running programs are unaffected by the change. Any programs started after you change mappings will inherit the new, changed mappings. This method of resource allocation allows you to have several DOS sessions running at the same time, each with a different set of drive mappings. Note that Windows itself and all Windows applications share the same set of resources.

If NWShare Handles is on, the Windows NetWare drivers use Global Resource Visibility, which means that a drive or printer mapping change made in one session immediately affects all other sessions. This setting is potentially disastrous if you routinely run several programs at once, because one program can remove or change another program's disk-drive mappings.

The second setting in the 386 Enhanced section, Restore Drives, is also related to drive mappings. Normally, any NetWare drive mappings created in Windows are discarded when you exit Windows. For example, if you start Windows and create a new drive G: from the Windows File Manager, then the G: drive will be unmapped when you exit Windows.

If you prefer, you can tell NetWare to leave the drive mappings as they are when you exit Windows. To do this, uncheck the Restore Drives check box.

The next three settings in the NetWare settings dialog box are related to network printing. On a very large network, there may be dozens or even hundreds of jobs waiting for a particular network printer. If you use the Print Manager to view pending network print jobs, the list of waiting jobs may become very long. The Maximum Jobs setting determines the maximum number of NetWare print jobs displayed in the Print Manager display window.

The next setting, Buffer Size, tells Windows how much memory space to allocate for each attached NetWare printer. A larger buffer (up to 30,000 bytes) increases print speed at the cost of additional memory consumption. The default setting of 3,500 bytes works well in most cases.

The final printer-related setting, Update Seconds, tells NetWare how often to update the Print Manager print-queue display. The default setting is 30 seconds; the range of allowable values is 1 through 65. Selecting a shorter interval updates the Print Manager display more often, but also causes a significant increase in network traffic, especially if there are many print jobs in the queue.

The last setting, Network Warning, alerts you to three network error conditions:

- The NetWare workstation software (MSIPX and NETX) was not loaded before Windows started.

- The IPX and/or NETX programs are older than the version recommended for use with Windows.

- There isn't enough free memory to load the Windows NetWare support modules.

If one of these error conditions exists when Windows starts, Windows will display an error message on the screen. To disable the error messages, uncheck the Network Warning check box.

Workstation Shell Options

There are two additional NetWare options that can't be controlled from the Control Panel. These additional settings reside in the SHELL.CFG workstation configuration file. The NetWare drivers load the options from the SHELL.CFG file when you load the NETX workstation driver, usually at system boot time.

The SHELL.CFG file is usually located in the root directory of your boot drive. SHELL.CFG is an optional file; your particular NetWare installation may not require it. If you don't have a SHELL.CFG file, you can create one with any text editor program. For optimal use with Windows, we recommend that you create a SHELL.CFG file with the following two settings:

```
FILE HANDLES=60
SHOW DOTS=ON
```

By default, NetWare reserves enough internal memory space to allow 40 open files at one time. If you're running Windows from a NetWare server, or if you're running several application programs over the network, 40 files may not be enough. The first line in our sample SHELL.CFG file, FILE HANDLES=60, tells NetWare to reserve space for 60 open files.

The second line, SHOW DOTS=ON, tells NetWare to display the current and parent directories as (.) and (..) in Windows. NetWare does not normally display the current and parent directories; most Windows applications use file list boxes, which show all the drives and directories available. Without the (.) and (..) display, it is impossible to navigate through a drive's directories. Setting SHOW DOTS=ON overcomes this problem.

If you prefer to place the SHELL.CFG file in a different directory, you can change the NETX command in your AUTOEXEC.BAT file to point to the file to use. The Windows SETUP program automatically places the NETX command in your AUTOEXEC.BAT, usually as the last item in the file. To use a different SHELL.CFG file, add **/C=***pathname* to the end of the NETX command, where pathname is the name of your workstation configuration file. For example, the command

```
NETX /C=C:\BIN\NWSHELL.CFG
```

tells NETX to use the file C:\BIN\NWSHELL.CFG.

Controlling NetWare from Windows

Before we dig into the details of running Windows with NetWare, it's important to understand some basic NetWare operations. In order to connect to a NetWare server from a DOS client, you typically follow these steps:

1. Load IPX and NETX from the DOS command line. After NETX loads, an additional drive letter appears on your system. This is the login drive, and it contains the NetWare LOGIN.EXE program.

2. Switch to the login drive and type LOGIN to start the login process.

3. Enter your user name and password when asked.

If the system administrator has defined a system-wide login script, the script will run. The script may create network drive and printer assignments. If you have defined a user login script, it will run after the system login script. Like the system-wide script, your own login script may create additional drive and printer assignments.

As you can see, there's a lot of room for variation here. Depending on your personal login script and the system login script, NetWare may or may not create any additional drive and printer connections when you log in to the network. If these connections do exist, Windows for Workgroups will keep them in place when Windows starts.

To make sure that the same NetWare drive and printer connections exist each time you start Windows for Workgroups, you should always log in to your NetWare network before you start Windows.

Adding and Removing NetWare Drives

NetWare drives operate just like other network drives. You add and remove NetWare drive mappings with the File Manager. To view, add, or change your NetWare drive mappings, follow these steps:

1. Start the File Manager by double-clicking on the File Manager icon.

2. Click on the Connect Network Drive icon ( ), or select Connect Network Drive from the Disk menu. Windows displays the Connect Network Drive dialog box. If you haven't logged in to the network, you'll be prompted to enter your user name and password.

3. Click on the NetWare button at the right side of the dialog box. The Network Drive Connections dialog box appears, as shown in Figure 7.2. Any existing NetWare drive assignments appear in the list of drives.

Figure 7.2

The Network Drive Connections dialog box shows any existing NetWare drive connections and allows you to add or delete additional drive connections.

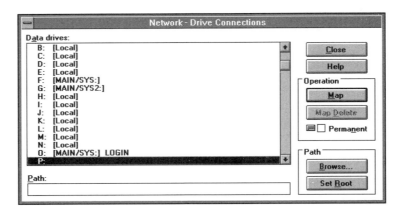

Using NetWare with Windows for Workgroups   **111**

To delete an existing drive mapping, follow these steps:

1. Select the drive letter you wish to delete.
2. Click on Map Delete to remove the drive mapping.

To add a new drive mapping, follow these steps:

1. Select the drive letter you wish to map. Note that the Data Drives display shows your current NetWare drive assignments but does not show current LAN Manager and/or Windows for Workgroups drive assignments.
2. If you're already logged in to the NetWare network and know the exact path name of the NetWare directory, type the full NetWare path name in the Path box and skip to step 7. You must include the full volume and directory name (for example, SYS:PUBLIC) even if your NetWare server has only one volume.
3. If you don't know the exact path name, or if you're not logged in to the NetWare LAN, click on the Browse button.
4. To log in to the NetWare network, click on the Attach button; enter the server name, your user name, and your password; and click on OK.
5. Click on a server volume to see the available directories on the volume. Figure 7.3 shows a NetWare server with two volumes.

Figure 7.3

The NetWare Browse feature allows you to scroll through a list of available subdirectories on the server(s). In this example, we have one NetWare server with two disk volumes on the server.

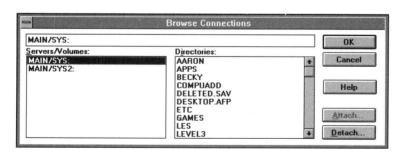

6. Select a network directory and click on OK.
7. If you want Windows to reconnect this drive each time you start Windows, click on the Permanent check box.
8. Click on the Map button to create the new drive mapping. To make the network drive appear as a root directory, select Set Root instead of Map.

9. If you want to connect more than one NetWare drive, go back to step 1 and repeat the process.

10. When you're finished mapping drives, click on the Close button.

NetWare Root Drive Mappings

NetWare drive mappings connect a logical drive letter to a specific directory on a network file server. When you select a network drive from the File Manager, the File Manager analyzes each network drive beginning at the root directory, *regardless of the drive's current mapping*. For example, if you have drive F: mapped to SYS:PUBLIC\APPS\WP51 and you select F: from the File Manager, the File Manager will scan the drive from the root directory.

This can cause several problems. First, it is annoying to have to wait for File Manager to read through the entire directory structure of the server. Second, while File Manager is reading the directory, it is creating a lot of unnecessary network traffic. Finally, you may not want to see the entire directory structure; usually you are interested in a specific network directory.

You can overcome these problems by using the Set Root button instead of the Map button when you set up your network drive mappings. Root-mapped drives appear to be at the top-level directory; any directories above the selected directory are hidden from DOS. As a result, File Manager runs faster and creates less network traffic.

Dueling Drives

As we just saw, the File Manager allows you to designate some or all of your Windows NetWare drive mappings as Permanent. While this is a convenient feature, it can lead to some problems. Specifically, Windows can't create a NetWare drive mapping unless you're logged in to the network.

When you install Windows for Workgroups, the Windows SETUP program adds the IPX and NETX commands to your AUTOEXEC.BAT file, thus establishing the connection to your NetWare login drive. However, Windows does not actually run the LOGIN program. If you boot your system and immediately start Windows, the login drive will appear as a network drive, but you will not be logged in to the NetWare network.

When Windows attempts to reconnect your Permanent NetWare drive mappings, it will fail because you aren't logged in to the NetWare LAN. To avoid this problem, you should always switch to your login drive and run LOGIN.EXE before you start Windows. If you have a login script on your NetWare server, the script may create drive mappings using the NetWare MAP command. These mappings will remain intact after you start Windows.

Using NetWare Printers

Connecting to a NetWare printer isn't much different from connecting to a Windows for Workgroups shared printer. As with Windows for Workgroups printers, you must have the correct printer driver installed on your PC before you can use a NetWare printer. For example, if your network has an HP LaserJet and an Apple LaserWriter, you'll need a separate Windows printer driver for each printer. See Chapter 4 for more details on installing printer drivers.

You connect your PC to a NetWare printer from the Printers module in the Control Panel or from the Print Manager program. To connect a network printer from the Control Panel, follow these steps:

1. Click on Printers in the Control Panel window.

2. Select the desired printer driver from the Installed Printers list and click on the Connect button. A list of existing printer connections appears.

3. Click on the Network button and the Connect Network Printer dialog box appears.

4. Ignore everything on this screen and click on the NetWare button.

5. If you're currently logged in to the NetWare network, a list of available network printer queues appears in the lower part of the window, as shown in Figure 7.4. If you're not logged in to the NetWare network, click on the Attach button, select a NetWare server, enter your user name and password, and then click on OK.

Figure 7.4

To establish a connection to a NetWare printer, you must choose a local printer port and assign the port to a network printer queue.

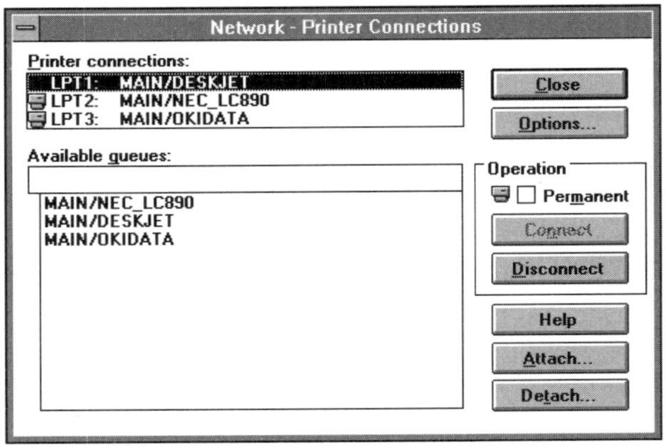

6. Select a printer port to use (choose from LPT1 through LPT3) and select a printer queue.

7. If you want Windows to reconnect this network printer each time you start Windows for Workgroups, click on the Permanent check box.

8. Click on Connect to complete the connection.

To connect to a NetWare printer from the Print Manager, follow these steps:

1. Start the Print Manager program by double-clicking on the Print Manager icon from the Windows desktop.

2. Select the Connect Network Printer option from the Printer pull-down menu or click on the Connect Network Printer icon ( ). The Connect Network Printer dialog box appears.

3. Follow the instructions under step 4 above.

You can also use the Print Manager to monitor your NetWare print jobs. We'll examine the Print Manager in detail in Chapter 11.

■ Using LAN Manager with Windows for Workgroups

Because Windows for Workgroups is based on Microsoft's LAN Manager product, the two products cooperate to provide nearly seamless networking. Resources on LAN Manager servers appear to Windows for Workgroups users as additional Windows for Workgroups shared disks and printers.

Conversely, DOS- and OS/2-based LAN Manager clients can access Windows for Workgroups shared resources using the standard LAN Manager workstation software. Unfortunately, Macintosh LAN Manager clients cannot access shared Windows for Workgroups resources.

Preparing to Use LAN Manager

Before you can use Windows for Workgroups to connect to a LAN Manager server, you must install the LAN Manager network driver. To install the driver, follow these steps:

1. Start Windows, open the Control Panel, and then double-click on the Network icon ( ). The Network Settings dialog box appears on the screen.

2. Click on the Networks icon ( ) at the bottom of the dialog box.

3. Select Microsoft LAN Manager from the list of supported networks and click on the Add button.

4. When asked, insert the floppy containing the LAN Manager drivers.

5. If you want to log in to the LAN Manager network automatically when you start Windows, click on the Log On to LAN Manager box and type the name of your LAN Manager server domain in the box.

6. Exit from the Control Panel, exit from Windows, and reboot your computer.

Using LAN Manager Drives and Printers

Once you install the LAN Manager driver, LAN Manager shared drives and printers appear in the File Manager, Print Manager, and Control Panel, just like Windows for Workgroups drives and printers. You connect to LAN Manager resources the same way you connect to Windows for Workgroups shared resources.

■ Sharing Files and Printers with Macintosh Computers

The Berlin Wall is gone. The Russians aren't Red anymore. Apple and IBM have formed a joint venture. And Mac users can share files with Windows users. Granted, the last one isn't quite as big a story as the first three—but if you work in an office with PCs and Macs, it may be the one that affects you the most.

In the early days of the Macintosh, communication with the PC universe ranged from difficult to impossible; Apple seemed to maintain a policy of deliberate incompatibility. As more Mac software vendors venture into the lucrative Windows marketplace (and vice versa), an interesting trend has developed. Today, many Macintosh applications can read and write files created by their Windows counterparts. Conversely, many Windows applications can read and write files in several Macintosh formats. For example, Microsoft's Word for Windows 2.0 can read files created by any version of Word for the Macintosh, and Word for the Macintosh version 5.0 can read and write Word for Windows files. WordPerfect, Page-Maker, Excel, Lotus 1-2-3, and many other applications provide similar capabilities. Programs with this kind of flexibility are ideal in a mixed-platform network.

Apple has taken a step toward improving Mac-to-PC connectivity by providing a PC-compatible 3½-inch floppy-disk drive in all recent Macs. The Apple SuperDrive can read and write 1.44-megabyte PC disks as well as native Mac format disks. If you need only occasional file transfers between your PCs and Macs, the SuperDrive may be all you need. Keep in mind, though, that the size of the largest file you can move on a floppy is limited to the size of the floppy disk itself.

Putting Macs on the Network

If your organization has a mixed bag of Macs and Windows machines, you may want to consider networking the machines together. There are a few hitches, though: Macintoshes can't connect to Windows for Workgroups PCs, and Macs can't operate as servers to PC clients. If you want to move files across the LAN between PCs and Macs, you'll need to add a server to your LAN.

Microsoft and Novell both offer add-on Macintosh connectivity solutions at an extra cost. These products provide file and printer sharing, and allow for the exchange of e-mail messages between PC and Macintosh users. Using these products, Macs can store files on the same servers with PCs, and all users can share the same printers. This makes life easier for everyone: Network managers can cover Mac and PC users with one backup, and network users can move files between the two platforms with no problem.

All Macs contain a built-in networking system called LocalTalk. LocalTalk is a 230 kilobit-per-second network that uses relatively inexpensive cable. To connect several Macs into a LocalTalk network, you must purchase a LocalTalk Connector Box for each Mac. The connector box is essentially a "Y" connector; the bottom of the "Y" connects to the Mac, and each side of the "Y" can connect to another connector box farther on down the cable. Several third-party vendors make alternative LocalTalk connectors that use standard modular telephone cable instead of Apple's shielded LocalTalk cable.

If your Macs are already connected to one another via LocalTalk, you can attach the LocalTalk network to your PC LAN file server via a LocalTalk board installed in the server. This allows the Macs to talk to the file server via LocalTalk while the PC users connect via Ethernet or Token-Ring. The only additional hardware expense is the cost of the LocalTalk board for the server. LocalTalk provides a serviceable, if not speedy, solution to the problem of how to let Macs and PCs share files and peripherals at a relatively low cost.

Keep in mind that graphics-based applications tend to create very large data files. If you'll need to move large files (like those created by PageMaker), you'll find that LocalTalk runs out of horsepower very quickly.

A better (but more expensive) alternative is to connect your Macs to your existing PC LAN. For example, if your PCs are connected via thin Ethernet, you can install an Ethernet adapter in each of your Macs. Ethernet runs at 10 megabits per second, or about 40 times the speed of LocalTalk. By putting all of your PCs and Macs on the same physical cable, you'll only have one cable to worry about. Macintosh Ethernet and Token-Ring boards are available from several vendors, including Shiva, Asanté, and Dayna Communications.

Whose File Is This?

Macintosh files are fundamentally different from their PC counterparts. Other than the three-character file name extension, DOS files don't contain any information to indicate what type of data they hold.

The Mac operating system maintains a directory of all files on every disk, much like DOS. But the Macintosh directory information is more comprehensive than the DOS directory. Every Mac file has a file type and a file-creator name associated with it. The Mac operating system uses this information to determine which application to start when the user double-clicks on the file's icon. The creator and type information also tells the Mac operating system which icon to associate with the file. Finally, Mac file names may be up to 31 characters long and may contain both upper- and lowercase letters, punctuation marks, and spaces. DOS file names are limited to the familiar eight-by-three format: an eight-character name followed by a three-character file type. DOS file types are completely arbitrary; software developers are free to choose whatever file extension they like for their application's files.

Over the years, a few standards have evolved; if you see a file named MAILING.DBF, you can be pretty sure it's a dBASE data file. On the other hand, if you see a file named REPORT.DOC, you can be fairly sure it's a word processor document—but you'll have to figure out which word processor created the file. Macintosh file and creator types are coordinated by Apple. When a developer wants to create a new file type, he or she contacts Apple, and Apple reserves a type and creator for that application.

This difference in naming structures brings up two issues. First, if PC and Mac users are to share the same files, then the same file must appear under two different names: one for PC users and one for Mac users. Second, in order for Mac users to access PC files, there must be some mechanism for converting DOS file-type information into a form meaningful to the Mac operating system.

NetWare and LAN Manager both automatically truncate long Mac file names into legal DOS file names, but they do it in slightly different fashions. As a test, we created two Word for Macintosh files called THIS IS A LONG FILE NAME and THIS IS A LONG FILE NAME, TOO. The table below shows how the two operating systems handled this challenge:

	LAN Manager	**NetWare**
File 1	THISISAL.ONG	THISISAL.
File 2	THISISAL.INE	THISISA0

Both operating systems discarded the comma and spaces because they're not allowed in DOS file names, and both converted the long Mac file name to a unique DOS file name.

LAN Manager includes a facility to map DOS file types to a specific Mac file type and creator. This allows DOS files to appear to Mac users by their familiar icons, and it allows Mac users to open a file by clicking on the icon. LAN Manager comes with a predefined list of file types and creators, and you can add your own to the list as necessary. Using this feature, the operating system automatically fills in the type and creator information as new DOS files are created on the network. NetWare for Macintosh lacks this feature. If you want DOS files to have a Mac creator and type under NetWare, you'll have to edit each individual file with ResEdit or a similar Mac file utility program.

Sharing Printers

First let's clear up the popular misconception that Apple LaserWriter printers can only print Macintosh files. In fact, LaserWriters are just plain-vanilla PostScript printers. There's nothing proprietary about them; you send them PostScript data, and they'll print a page for you.

In fact, the original LaserWriter was the first PostScript printer on the market. Many PostScript printers from other manufacturers include the same set of fonts as the Apple printers in order to maintain complete "plug and play" compatibility with Apple's printers. The very early LaserWriters didn't have a parallel port and weren't widely used in the PC universe. Later models added a parallel port, and the newest models also include a SCSI port.

In an all-Apple world, most LaserWriters (or compatibles) are connected to their host Macs via LocalTalk. LocalTalk (originally called AppleTalk) was originally designed to let several Mac users share one or more LaserWriters.

LAN Manager and NetWare both provide a facility to share PostScript printers among all LAN users. This lets PC users gain access to formerly Mac-only PostScript printers, and it allows Mac users to print on any other PostScript printers attached to the network. Instead of printing directly to the printer, all users print to a network printer queue. The server holds incoming print jobs in order in the queue and sends them to the printer on a first-in first-out basis. This allows users to go about their work while the server waits for the printer. The printers themselves may attach to the server via LocalTalk, or you can use serial or parallel connections to hook the printers to the server.

- *Windows × LANs × Applications = Challenge*
- *Microsoft Word 2.0 and Excel 4.0*
- *Microsoft PowerPoint Version 3.0*
- *Lotus 1-2-3 for Windows and Ami Pro*
- *WordPerfect for Windows*
- *Networked DDE: A Tutorial*

CHAPTER

Applications and Windows for Workgroups

A COMPUTER OR A COMPUTER NETWORK DOESN'T CONTRIBUTE much to your productivity without application software. Electronic mail and scheduling are productivity enhancers, but people depend on the traditional functions of spreadsheet, word processing, database, graphics, and communications programs to get their work done.

A discussion of how to use applications under Windows for Workgroups has two distinct parts: (1) setting up the applications and file structures, and (2) using the networked DDE (Dynamic Data Exchange) that is such a unique part of the network operating system's appeal. We'll begin this chapter with an overview of how programs share resources and what they look for across the network. Then we'll discuss the installation and operation of some specific programs. We'll describe how to integrate the applications into the network and how to point the programs toward their shared files and printers. Finally, we'll provide a step-by-step tutorial illustrating how to use the networked DDE service.

■ Windows × LANs × Applications = Challenge

Installing applications under Windows involves one set of problems. Installing applications on networks involves a separate set of problems. Unfortunately, when you install Windows applications on a network, the effects of the two sets of problems don't add together—they multiply. Fortunately, Microsoft spent the time between the release of Windows 3.1 and the release of Windows for Workgroups tracking down problems and educating programmers who want to develop applications for both environments. As a result, modern applications literally load themselves when they are used in normal configurations and when they detect standard environments. But the normal conditions and standard environments of real networks are not always what Microsoft and application developers would like them to be.

You will typically run into installation problems involving two things: paths and drivers. Windows programs need a lot of configuration information each time they start up. Some older Windows programs store this information in a WIN.INI file on each PC. This leads to the creation of large WIN.INI files that become complex and obsolete and slow down the start up of Windows. Modern programs create their own separate .INI files in the Windows subdirectory, although they might still put pointers to those files into WIN.INI. If the program can't find the path to its configuration files, the results can vary from urgent messages flashed on the screen during start up to total failure of the program. Failures severe enough to freeze Windows 3.1 are increasingly rare, but they can happen.

In theory, Windows provides all the needed video, keyboard, and input/output port drivers for every application; that is one advantage of the comprehensive Windows environment. But the theory doesn't always work. Some installation programs modify your SYSTEM.INI file by adding DEVICE= statements pointing to specific drivers, which are usually contained in the WINDOWS\SYSTEM subdirectory. Different PC configurations require different video board, keyboard, and printer drivers. If a program can't find the right device driver for the PC it is running in, it might not display, print, or communicate properly. When a program loads across a network or when you try to use a program without following the installation process for each PC, chances are good that the program won't find all the configuration files and drivers it needs.

HINT. *It is very difficult to uninstall Windows applications, but unused applications can swell your .INI files, consume memory, and slow the system's operation. Make copies of your CONFIG.SYS, AUTOEXEC.BAT, WIN.INI, and SYSTEM.INI files before you install a major application and save those files on a carefully labeled floppy. When you no longer need the application, you can use a word processor to examine each file as it appeared both before and after the installation. Then, you can find and delete lines added by the application's installation program.*

Our Best Advice

If you want to create a network that will operate reliably, here is our best advice: Give each networked client PC at least 8 megabytes of memory along with a hard-disk drive of at least 130 megabytes and then install each application separately on each PC. Configure the network to store data files on servers while storing application programs on each PC. We recommend putting a master copy of each program's installation files on a server so you only have to read in the floppies once. But keep the configured programs on each PC to reduce network traffic and overall complexity.

Our recommended hardware configuration will give you enough hard-disk drive space to install application programs separately on each PC. Mating Windows programs to specific PCs is important because these programs record critical details about the paths they use to find their configuration files, printer and screen drivers, and other resources. It is very difficult to get these details correct if you don't let each installation program do its own work on each PC. If you mount 300- or 600-megabyte drives in a few PCs and use them as servers for data files, you will keep network traffic down, reduce complexity, and improve security.

The primary alternative to our recommended approach is to put one copy of each application program onto a shared hard-disk drive and then to use that single copy of the program on every networked PC. Under this configuration, when you click on an icon to start an application, Windows for Workgroups pulls the program across the network and into your PC to run it. This approach often worked for DOS programs, but it is much less successful for Windows programs. It takes careful installation and planning to ensure that a Windows program pulled across the network from a server can find its .INI files and appropriate hardware drivers when it runs on a specific PC.

Some people argue that a network configured so that each station pulls a single copy of an application from a shared server is easier to administer. Certainly it is easier to update that single copy of the program, but the other administrative burdens are just as complex. You'll probably need to dedicate a separate subdirectory on the server to each person; this subdirectory will contain all the needed .INI files and drivers for every program. When you concentrate all this data on the centralized server, you have a single point of failure. If that server holding your primary applications malfunctions, everyone on the LAN is out of luck. But if people have their own adequate hard-disk drive storage and their own copies of applications, they can still get work done even if the entire network is not functioning.

Unfortunately, our recommended reliable system configuration requires a somewhat larger up-front investment per PC than other alternatives. However, we believe that selecting the network configuration is a pay-me-now or pay-me-later decision. The lower initial cost of installing PCs without enough hard-disk storage to hold all their applications is deceiving. If you drag programs, particularly large and complex Windows programs, from a shared disk drive across the network, you will have a much busier network with slower response time and more failures. You'll spend your time chasing transient problems and working with less-than-satisfied customers instead of promoting workgroup efficiency through the use of interactive applications.

Another significant drawback to pulling programs into each PC from a shared drive across the network is that you must contend with the legal and moral issues of software licensing. Although it is possible to carry the same copy of a program to each PC and install it, that sin of commission is less likely than the sin of omission found in installations where the program files are held on a central server. It is easy, although still illegal, to turn your head and let another person use an improperly licensed program on a file server.

It is generally agreed within the industry that organizations that don't or can't buy a site license or a network license for their software are still within the spirit of the law if they purchase a copy of the software for each user. Even if they simply stack the unused floppies in a closet and share a single copy of the program across the network, they have paid the developing company its due. (We've seen companies with closets full of unopened software packages!) But the temptation to buy just a single copy of the program and to illegally share it across the network is strong. Microsoft's standard licensing agreement says that "...you must have a reasonable mechanism or process in place to assure that the number of persons using the SOFTWARE does not exceed the number of Licenses."

No Floppy Drives

If cost is an extremely important factor in planning your network configuration, we suggest you consider trading off floppy drives for hard-disk drives. If two floppy drives add 5 percent to the price of a PC, it would be better to have no floppy drives and spend the money on a larger hard-disk drive for each PC. Xinetron is one company that offers powerful PCs with internal hard-disk drives, integrated LAN adapters, but no floppy drives.

Many corporate managers view having floppy drives on every PC as a disadvantage for two reasons: security and the computer virus threat. In many organizations the data on the network—client records, market research, cost models, and custom software—is a corporate asset. If someone walks out the door with a 1.44-megabyte floppy of client data, the organization can suffer serious economic harm. It is easier to keep data secure if people don't have floppy drives on their PCs.

Viruses are a real threat to workgroup data and efficiency. Modern, sophisticated viruses do their work without advertising their presence on the screen. Virus-caused problems that steal productivity can appear to be hardware faults or unexplained software quirks. We don't know of a virus that can travel across a network in data files, but they do travel very well in executable files and on bootable floppies. If people don't have floppy drives on their PCs, they can't introduce viruses into the system.

We think it is best to install each application on each PC, but this doesn't mean that each PC needs its own floppy drive. You can install and update software in several ways on PCs that don't have their own floppy drives. We'll assume that a hard-disk drive in a new PC comes loaded with a bootable operating system or that you can initialize a new drive in an existing PC and load an operating system to get started.

Even if you are faced with a PC that has no floppy drives and displays only the C: prompt on the screen, you can use a laptop PC and a product such as Traveling Software's Lap-Link to load the Windows for Workgroups files into that machine's hard-disk drive. After the files are loaded, typing **SETUP** starts the ten-minute process of creating a fully capable Windows for Workgroups machine.

If someone must have access to a floppy drive for a specific purpose, remember that Windows for Workgroups allows you to share any networked drive. You can make the floppy drives in the administrator's PC or in an installer's portable PC available as shared drives across the LAN. The network connection is so much faster than the data retrieval rate of the floppy drive that you won't see a performance difference between an internal floppy drive and one shared across the network.

Easy Installation

Once you have Windows for Workgroups running, you can pull installation files for applications across the network. That process is a lot easier than hand-feeding the installation floppies into each PC. First, check to see if the program provides an automated way to load the floppies on a networked PC. As we explained in Chapter 3, even Windows for Workgroups offers an option for installation from a server with the SETUP/A command.

If the program doesn't offer an automated installation on the server, here's what you should do. First, create a shared subdirectory clearly designated as holding the installation files; F:\WORDINST is a good example. Then use the XCOPY command in DOS to move all the files from each floppy to that subdirectory. If the floppy is in the A: drive and your PC's path is set to search the DOS subdirectory, then the format of the command is

```
XCOPY A:\ F:\WORDINST /s /e
```

The /s and /e commands tell XCOPY to copy all subdirectories, even empty ones. Copy each installation floppy into the shared subdirectory.

Many installation floppy sets have a small ASCII file on each floppy with the name of the floppy, such as DISK3. Some programs look for these small files, so don't erase them if they come across into the installation subdirectory.

Next, move to the PC where you want to install the program. Start Windows for Workgroups, but don't start any other applications. Connect the PC to the shared drive containing the installation subdirectory using File Manager and note the disk drive letter File Manager assigns.

Then, from the Windows Program Manager screen, pull down the File menu and select the Run option. When the dialog box shown in Figure 8.1 appears, type the full drive letter and path name for the installation program. You'll have to check the documentation for the name of the installation program. Microsoft typically uses SETUP as the name of its installation programs, while Lotus programs such as 1-2-3 for Windows and Ami Pro use INSTALL. In our example using Microsoft Word, you type F:\WORDINST\SETUP.EXE. The installation program will search your WIN.INI for signs of previous versions of the application program and to find the subdirectories holding .INI files, drivers, and DLLs. Then the program will ask you where you want to install the application.

At this point you can choose any available drive or subdirectory. But if you choose a networked drive to hold the installed program, make sure that it won't be overwritten by subsequent installations from other PCs. Also carefully consider the negative impact on performance and reliability caused by drawing a large program across the LAN each time you want to run it.

Figure 8.1

This dialog box appears after you select the Run option from File pull-down menu in the Program Manager. When you install applications, enter the full path name for the appropriate installation program.

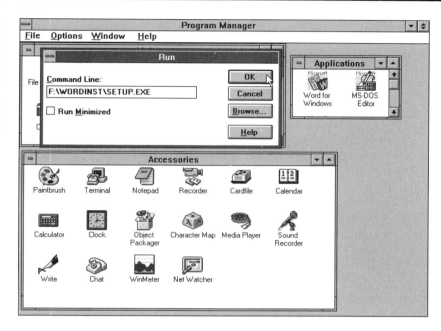

The installation program will configure your PC's WIN.INI and might make changes to SYSTEM.INI, CONFIG.SYS, and AUTOEXEC.BAT. It will also write its own .INI file and any needed .386, .DLL, or .FON files in appropriate subdirectories during the installation process.

Using Files on the Network

After the initial installation of a program, you typically must point an application to its data files and attach it to any shared printers. Using data files on a shared network drive can be tricky because people can lose their work if the programs don't follow the proper conventions for opening and closing files across the network. For that reason, we suggest giving each person a private, password-protected subdirectory on a server for file storage. But there are times when people must access the same documents, database files, and spreadsheets without having multiple copies tucked away in each individual's file space.

Modern programs typically open a data file using instructions that tell the file-handling system, either DOS or a DOS-like network operating system, to prevent other applications from changing the file while the first application has it open. If this first-come, first-served protection is not in effect, then two people could open and make different changes to the same file at

Chapter 8: Applications and Windows for Workgroups

the same time, but the changes made by the last person to close the file would overwrite the changes made by the first person to close the file. Overwriting simultaneously changed files is a problem typically associated with older DOS applications, but you should be alert for it.

In modern applications, if two people try to open the same data file at the same time, the second person will receive read-only access. The second and subsequent simultaneous users can see the file and make changes to it, but they must save the changed files under different file names.

As Figure 8.2 illustrates, some programs, such as Microsoft Word, can tell you the name of the person on the network who has the file open. In this case Word doesn't get the person's name from the network, but from information left by the copy of the program that opened the file. The user name shown is the name registered in the Word program, not in the network operating system. Not many programs are so informative.

Figure 8.2

In Microsoft Word, the second person trying to simultaneously open a file receives notification that the file is already open. The name of the person using the file comes from the name registered in the Word program, not from the user name in the network.

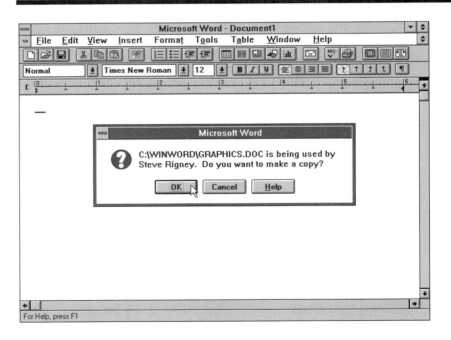

Some programs, specifically database systems, are designed to allow multiple applications to simultaneously read and write in the same data file. These programs don't instruct DOS to lock a file when they open it, but they use more detailed techniques to lock a range of bytes in the program, generally referred to as a record, while it is being read and written.

Sharing Printers

In Chapter 4, we described how to share printers and how to attach to shared printers. But you'll have to point each application that needs printer access to the correct printer port, set it up for the correct type of printer, and, if the program comes with its own drivers, decide between the application's drivers and those in Windows.

After you select one or more shared printers using Print Manager, you must take several actions in the Windows Control Panel to make shared printers available to application programs. Double-clicking on the Printers icon in the Control Panel and click on the Connect button to display a list, shown in Figure 8.3, of the available ports selected through Print Manager. Clicking on the Network button allows you to select other available network printers. This function works like Print Manager.

Figure 8.3

The Connect dialog box shows you a list of printers available under Windows. You can click on the Network button to see all networked printers.

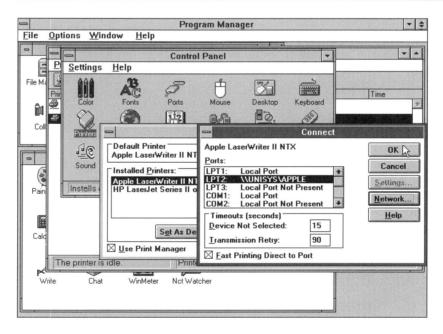

It can be important to properly assign specific LPT ports to certain locally attached printers and to certain printers used across the network. While Windows for Workgroups will allow you to assign LPT1, LPT2, and LPT3 to a printer, some programs, typically older DOS programs, will not address all those ports. You might have to plan carefully to associate the printer a program needs with an LPT port it can address. Windows programs allow you to select a specific printer each time you select the Print option from the pull-down File menu, but you should have a primary (also called default) setup.

■ Microsoft Word 2.0 and Excel 4.0

The network installation steps for Microsoft Word version 2.0 and for Microsoft Excel version 4.0 are practically identical. We will use Word as the example; except for the name you might choose to give the subdirectory, the process is the same.

You can install Word so that all the program files reside on each PC, or you can pull files across the network from a server for execution, but pulling the files across the network is the slower and less reliable method.

Microsoft recommends letting the SETUP program copy all the files to the appropriate hard-disk drive. For the first installation, you should work from a PC that is a client to a Windows for Workgroups server and not from the server itself. The first step is to pull down the File menu in Program Manager and select the Run option. Then, with the disk labeled Setup–Disk 1 in the A drive, type **A:\SETUP**. Follow the screen instructions until you come to the box that suggests where the Word program files should reside. Designate a path (including subdirectory name) on the server. At this point, SETUP checks for available hard-disk drive space and presents the options shown in Figure 8.4.

During the first installation of the program on the network, click on the Server Installation button. This selection leads to a series of steps that transfers the files from the installation floppies to a directory you can use for subsequent installations. This isn't a complete installation, and the program isn't fully configured, but the files are ready for individual installation on each client PC.

During the subsequent installation of Word on client PCs, run the SETUP program from the drive on the server. You could, for example, enter E:\WINWORD\SETUP in the Run menu under File or double-click on the SETUP.EXE program in the appropriate drive display in File Manager. When the SETUP program asks where you want the Word files, enter a path on your local hard-disk drive or in a private subdirectory on a server. Then, instead of the Server Installation button, SETUP will display a button labeled Workstation Installation, shown in Figure 8.5. Choose this button to complete the installation.

SETUP will take files from the original subdirectory on the server and efficiently move them to their destination. It will modify your AUTOEXEC.BAT files and WIN.INI to point to the installed files. It will also install VER.DLL, SHELL.DLL, OLECLI.DLL, and OLESVR.DLL into the WINDOWS\SYSTEM subdirectory, so be sure that you have full rights to that subdirectory.

Microsoft Word 2.0 and Excel 4.0 **131**

Figure 8.4

This Microsoft Word installation menu provides the option of choosing a server installation. This option moves the installation files to a shared drive on a server, but does not complete a fully configured installation. You must run SETUP from each networked PC to complete the installation.

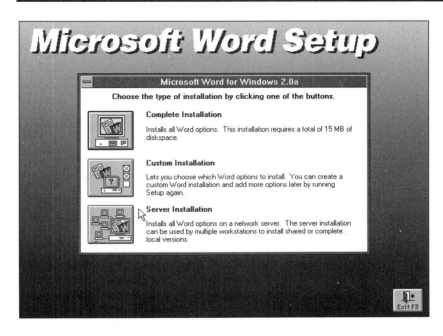

Figure 8.5

After the SETUP program transfers the installation files to a shared subdirectory, the SETUP menu offers these three installation options. Choose the Workstation Installation button to install the program from the server drive and to avoid handling the floppies again.

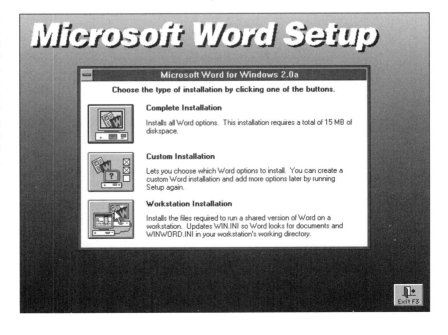

Chapter 8: Applications and Windows for Workgroups

It's easy to take advantage of shared network drives and printers through Microsoft Word. If you select the Open command from the File pull-down menu in Word, you'll see the Drives list in the Open dialog box shown in Figure 8.6. For networked drives, this box lists the drive letter and the file server and shared directory name. The presentation of this detailed information makes it easy to find the correct shared drive. The Print Setup command, also available from the File pull-down menu in Word, displays a list of locally attached and networked printers (Figure 8.7). These printers are installed into Windows using the Printer functions of the Control Panel as described earlier in this chapter and in Chapter 4.

Figure 8.6

The Drives list contains a selection of drive letters and associated server names and shared directories.

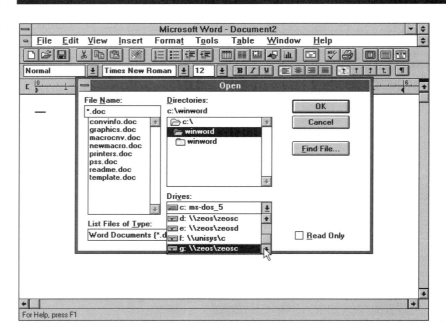

■ Microsoft PowerPoint Version 3.0

Microsoft uses its newest procedure for running SETUP and installing applications on networked drives in both Windows for Workgroups and PowerPoint version 3.0. As we described in Chapter 3, you can choose to run the SETUP program with either of two command line switches: /A or /N. Typing SETUP/A tells the program to transfer the files from the installation floppies to a shared subdirectory on the server. You type SETUP/N to use those server-based installation files to create a working copy of PowerPoint on each networked PC. You can direct the installation program to put the configured program files in a local drive or in a subdirectory on the server, but pulling executable files across the network increases network traffic and reduces reliability.

The printer setup and installation procedures for PowerPoint are the same as for Microsoft Word and Excel.

Figure 8.7

Selecting Print Setup from the File pull-down menu in Word allows you to select from all the local and networked printers. The Apple LaserWriter on LPT2 is a printer physically attached to another networked PC and shared across the network.

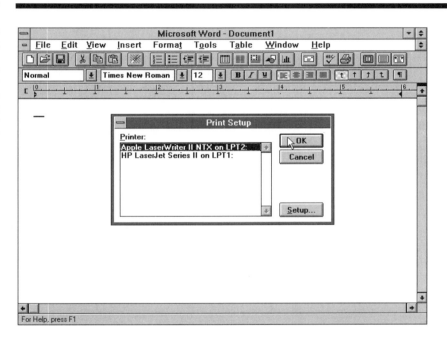

■ Lotus 1-2-3 for Windows and Ami Pro

The Lotus Ami Pro word processing program provides excellent flexibility with some unique features. Our favorite Ami Pro feature lets you insert in-text editing notes in the form of yellow "Post-it" notes. Ami Pro also excels in its ability to import and export text to many other word processing programs, making it a good choice for mixed-platform offices. Lotus 1-2-3 for Windows is a Windows version of the well-known spreadsheet program. Both Ami Pro and 1-2-3 for Windows use a similar program called INSTALL, which provides options for moving files to the server and performing a complete installation.

You begin the installation of Ami Pro or 1-2-3 for Windows by running the Lotus INSTALL program from the Run dialog box of the File pull-down menu in Program Manager. Typically, you'll type **A:\INSTALL** to start the program from a floppy on the A: drive. The latest versions of INSTALL offer an option button, shown in Figure 8.8, for a network server installation. If you choose this option, INSTALL moves the installation files to a shared subdirectory on a server's drive. When you want to install Ami Pro on a networked PC, you run INSTALL from the shared subdirectory, as in

```
E:\AMIPRO\INSTALL
```

The INSTALL program will ask you where you want to install the configured program files and complete the installation.

Figure 8.8

The latest versions of the INSTALL program used by Lotus in Ami Pro and 1-2-3 for Windows provide an option button for server installation. Selecting this option moves the installation files to a networked subdirectory. In subsequent installations, you run INSTALL from the subdirectory to create a fully configured program.

You select printers for these applications by pulling down the File menu and clicking on the Print Setup option. The shared and local printers made available through the Printers module of the Control Panel appear for selection in the same way that they do in the Microsoft programs described above. But the Lotus programs do not provide the same detailed description of the shared disk-drive resources found in the Microsoft programs. The Lotus programs show you all the available drive letters, but nothing else. You must know the DOS drive letter associated with a specific shared server resource.

■ WordPerfect for Windows

The installation program for WordPerfect for Windows looks and acts like the same program used for the DOS version of WordPerfect. You cannot run WordPerfect's INSTALL.EXE program from Windows, even in a DOS window. You must run it from the DOS prompt. The menu offers an option for network installation, but this option primarily allows you to tell the WordPerfect program what type of network operating system you have so it can establish some communication between programs running on the network.

The WordPerfect installation program creates, among other things, three environment files called WP{WP}.ENV, WPC.INI, and WPC_NET.INI. These files contain personalized options for each user. WP{WP}.ENV resides in the main WordPerfect installation directory, typically called WPWIN. The .INI files are in the Windows subdirectory.

WP{WP}.ENV is very important to the proper operation of the program. It is just a simple text file that is originally set up by INSTALL.EXE, but you can edit it using the Windows Notepad program or any other ASCII text editor. As Figure 8.9 illustrates, the INSTALL program asks you what brand of networking software you intend to use. Because Windows for Workgroups is not on the menu, we suggest using the entry for 3Com 3+ Open, an early form of the LAN Manager software using the SMB and NetBEUI protocols. A line of text beginning with the characters /NT= in the WP{WP}.ENV file lists the network number entered through INSTALL.

Figure 8.9

When WordPerfect's INSTALL program asks you what networking software you are using, we suggest you choose option B, 3Com 3+ Open.

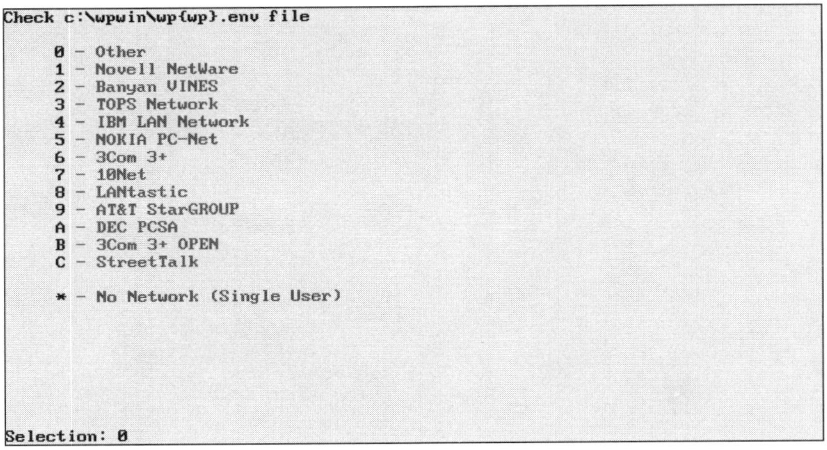

```
Check c:\wpwin\wp{wp}.env file

    0 - Other
    1 - Novell NetWare
    2 - Banyan VINES
    3 - TOPS Network
    4 - IBM LAN Network
    5 - NOKIA PC-Net
    6 - 3Com 3+
    7 - 10Net
    8 - LANtastic
    9 - AT&T StarGROUP
    A - DEC PCSA
    B - 3Com 3+ OPEN
    C - StreetTalk

    * - No Network (Single User)


Selection: 0
```

Chapter 8: Applications and Windows for Workgroups

A line of text beginning with /WPC= in the WP{WP}.ENV file tells the program where to look for its files. This is a useful entry when you are running the program from across the network. You can enter a line beginning with /PS= to tell the program where to find your personal configuration files. You might change this entry if you want to keep files on a local drive. The /NI= entry tells the program where to look for its .INI files. This parameter is necessary if the .INI files aren't in a directory included in your PC's path.

WordPerfect for Windows is one of the few Windows programs that comes with printer driver software that you can elect to use instead of the drivers contained in Windows. Figure 8.10 shows WordPerfect's Select Printer dialog box, available from the Print Setup option of the File pull-down menu. This dialog box is used to select the WordPerfect drivers instead of the Windows drivers. Many users report receiving better throughput for their print jobs when they select WordPerfect drivers. If WordPerfect has drivers available for your printers, it is worth trying them.

WordPerfect for Windows does not provide you with any detailed information about the identity of networked printers or disk drives. You must remember what LPT port is associated with a specific printer on the network and what DOS drive letter connects you to a specific server.

Figure 8.10

The WordPerfect Select Printer dialog box provides the option of using the program's own printer drivers instead of those in Windows. Many users report better throughput for their print jobs with the WordPerfect drivers, so this option is worth trying.

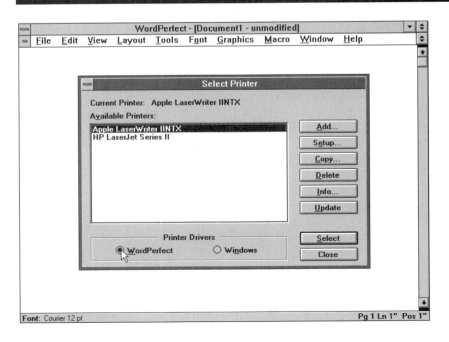

■ Networked DDE: A Tutorial

The Dynamic Data Exchange (DDE) feature has been a standard part of Windows since version 2.0. On stand-alone PCs, DDE allows Windows-based applications to exchange information. Pieces of data clipped from the work being prepared in an application, referred to as objects, can be shared between applications on the same PC.

The networked DDE feature of Windows for Workgroups allows people throughout an organization to share objects across a network. These objects can contain charts, drawings, digitized images, or pieces of text. An object created and made available for sharing by one person can be pasted simultaneously into the work of several other people across the network. Networked DDE works between different applications on different machines and between the same application on different machines.

You use the standard Copy and Paste commands from the Edit pull-down menu of your Windows-based application to share and to use shared objects. You can paste a shared chart or drawing into your work one time so it is permanent and unchanging, or you can paste it into your work with what is called a *hot link* back to the originating application. This hot link keeps the pasted object alive; as the originator of the original object updates and changes it, the pasted and linked copy in your work changes too.

This networked DDE capability is useful for all types of workgroup information-sharing activities. For example, people preparing a group's report can divide the tasks of making slides, entering data, creating spreadsheet graphs, and preparing a written report. The group preparing spreadsheet graphs can add last-minute data, and all the portions of the report will still agree, because each graph created in the spreadsheet program is linked into its own specific spot in the presentation and word processing programs. Similarly, people working on a design project can easily exchange drawings and charts through networked DDE.

Networked DDE can be used to generate slide presentations across a network for training and briefings, to control and update versions of documents and drawings across a network, and to play spectacular games. It opens significant opportunities in the areas of virtual reality and real-time interaction through stories or group activities. In the social sciences, applications using network DDE can be useful for role-playing, brainstorming, problem solving, and many other activities. The power of the linked programs will promote a high degree of group interaction. As we explain in Chapter 9, through remote communications people can participate in this interaction from the next office or even from another continent.

Clipboards and ClipBooks

Networked DDE actions can be programmed into an application so they are automatic and invisible, or they can operate through menu selections. The designers of games, for example, may give their creations the ability to automatically link and exchange data. Some programs, such as the Crosstalk communications program and the Excel spreadsheet program, contain their own programming or macro languages that can be used to establish automatic links across the network. Microsoft provides the Dynamic Data Exchange Management Library (DDEML) as a dynamic-link library for programmers. But many people will link their spreadsheets, graphics, and word processing programs across the network using the Windows Clipboard and the Windows for Workgroups ClipBook, which are available through the menus.

The Windows Clipboard is a buffer that holds segments of text, drawings, or graphics that you cut or copy from your work. You use the Paste command to move those segments from the buffer into other documents or presentations in the same program or in other Windows programs. Every Windows program offers the Cut, Copy, and Paste commands under the Edit pull-down menu shown in Figure 8.11.

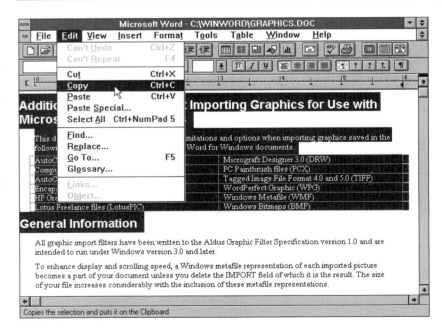

Figure 8.11

This screen from Microsoft Word shows the Cut, Copy, and Paste commands, which move specified segments of text, drawings, graphics, or pictures in and out of the Windows Clipboard. You cut or copy elements into the Clipboard and paste elements from the Clipboard into your work. This capability makes it easy to move and copy elements between Windows applications.

The ClipBook has two parts: a ClipBook server and the ClipBook Viewer. Together, these products form a communications exchange system that allows you to share objects across a network in the same way you share drives and printers. ClipBook servers communicate through the NetBIOS programming interface to the NetBEUI transport software. The servers use the network to make ClipBook objects, or *pages*, available for sharing. After you copy a segment of text or graphics into the local Clipboard, it requires a separate action to copy it from the Clipboard to the ClipBook. Then you share the pages of the ClipBook with people across the network. When you initiate the sharing function, you have several security options including password protection.

The people who want to use the shared ClipBook pages link to a specific PC's name through a ClipBook Viewer, select the desired page, and move it to the local Clipboard with a Copy command. Then, from within an application, the Paste or Paste Special command moves a segment of text or graphics into the work being created in the local Windows application. Figure 8.12 illustrates the process.

Figure 8.12

The process of making a DDE link across the network involves a local Windows Clipboard, a holding buffer, and the Windows for Workgroups ClipBook—a network object exchange mechanism—on each PC.

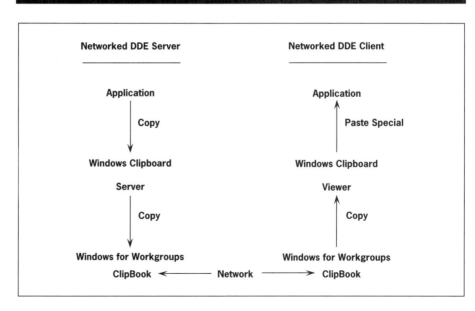

Networked DDE and OLE

You have probably heard about the Windows feature called *object linking and embedding* (OLE). The difference between OLE and DDE has become fuzzy. Object linking is analogous to using DDE. It allows you to paste information as a link from one application to another and to have the destination document dynamically updated to reflect changes made to the information in the source document.

Object embedding provides a way for information to be embedded, or directly inserted, into the destination document. Object embedding is different from linking in two ways. First, the information embedded at the destination consists not only of a representation of the object, such as a chart, but also of all the data used to create the object, such as the values in the underlying spreadsheet cells. Second, the embedded object is not updated dynamically; to update it, the user must double-click on the object.

Selected data elements that support embedding use a format that ends with the word "object," as in Excel Worksheet Object. But this type of object is useful only for embedding; do not attempt to paste this type of object into a document if you want to create a hot link. This difference is illustrated in the step-by-step instructions below.

At the practical level, OLE is built on top of DDE. Networked DDE seems to largely ignore the fine line and generalizes the functions for all DDE-capable applications.

Step by Step

We'll illustrate the process of sharing by linking a chart between two networked PCs. In our example, a person at the first PC, called the DDE server, will generate the chart using the Microsoft Excel spreadsheet. The person working on the second PC, called the DDE client, will link to the shared chart and paste it into a Microsoft Word document.

The first step is to designate the text or graphic element you want to link. In some programs you'll find a Select command under a pull-down menu; it's on the Chart pull-down menu in the Excel Chart window. In some programs, such as Paintbrush, you click on an object to select it. In word processing programs and spreadsheets, you drag the cursor across words or cells while holding down the left mouse button to select them. Drawing programs typically offer a function under a scissors icon that you can use to designate the portion of a picture or drawing you want to select. After you have selected the element, choose Copy from the Edit pull-down menu, as shown in Figure 8.13. This action moves the object into the Windows Clipboard.

Figure 8.13

We created this chart from an Excel spreadsheet. We selected the chart by clicking on it with the left mouse button. After selecting the element, we pulled down the Edit menu and selected the Copy option.

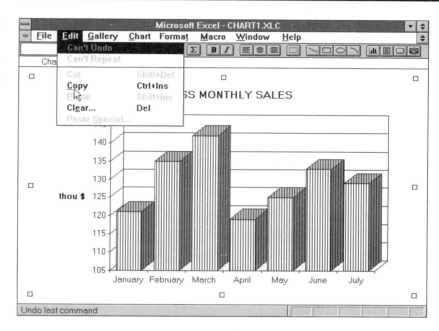

After copying the object into the Clipboard, activate the ClipBook by selecting its icon from the Main group in the Program Manager:

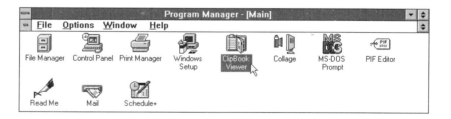

Choose the Paste command from the ClipBook Viewer's Edit menu so that you can paste the object from the Clipboard into the ClipBook:

In the Paste dialog box, enter a name or description for the information you have selected to paste. Select the Share Item Now box:

When you click on OK, the Share ClipBook Page dialog box appears. If you want real-time updates of the shared object, select the Start Application on Connect option. You can restrict access to the ClipBook item with a password:

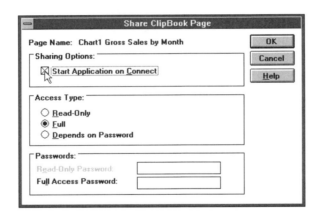

The object is now available in the ClipBook Viewer to any authorized PC running Windows for Workgroups:

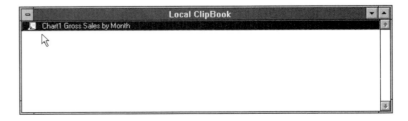

To link the object to a Microsoft Word document on another networked PC, first select the ClipBook Viewer on the second PC. When the ClipBook window opens, select the Connect command from the File menu. You must take this step whether or not you are already connected to the originating machine as a file, print, or mail server:

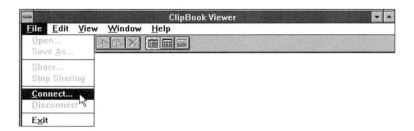

The Select Computer dialog box prompts you for a computer name. Select a computer from the Computers list or type in the correct computer name:

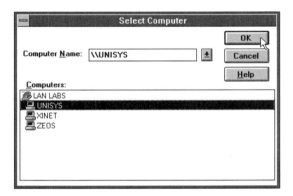

Then select the Copy command from the Edit menu. The selected object is copied from the ClipBook into the local Clipboard:

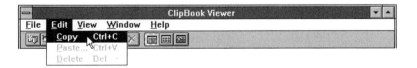

To bring the object into the document or presentation, switch to the application, place the cursor where you want to insert the object, and select Paste Special from the Edit menu:

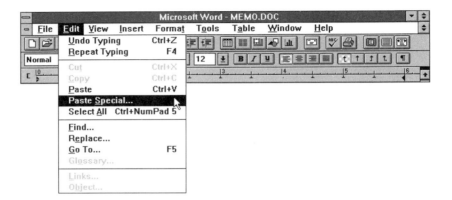

In the Paste Special dialog box, choose a format from the list and then click on either Paste or Paste Link. The Paste option will place a read-only version of the object into your application. The Paste Link option will place a pointer to the object into your document, along with a link back to the application used to create it. With Paste Link, all changes made to the object will be reflected immediately in your document:

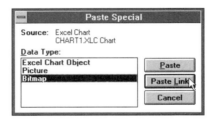

Note that Excel Chart Object is a special type of object that does not allow a hot link back to the originating application. If you select Excel Chart Object, the Paste Link button will be unavailable.

The chart, created in Excel, now appears in Microsoft Word (Figure 8.14). Other people on the network can also link to the chart from within different applications. As the chart is changed in Excel, the changed image appears in all of the documents linked to the chart.

Figure 8.14

The chart in this Microsoft Word for Windows document was created in Excel by another user and pasted into Word via the Windows for Workgroups ClipBook.

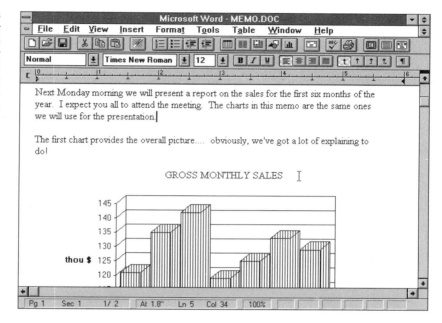

- *Dialing In*
- *Dialing Out*

CHAPTER 9

Network Communications

Networks are for sharing. But people often want to share a network's resources from wherever they might be, not just from within an office with a LAN. Devices called *access servers* provide a way for people to share a network's resources from anywhere there is a telephone line. A calling PC, equipped with a modem, can connect to an access server and use the services of a network.

Since modems with 9.6 and 14.4 kilobit-per-second signaling rates have reached economical price levels, dial-in network services have become very popular. Access servers extend a LAN to people working from home, a hotel, or another office. People can work at home during times of temporary absence, and the increasingly popular telecommuting option is more viable. Through an access server, remote callers can use a LAN's e-mail and access data files. Except for slower responsiveness to commands, dial-in service lets you use a network the same way you do in the office.

Remote printing is another cost-effective use of remote LAN access. Instead of printing a document in your office and then using an expensive overnight carrier to get it to the company headquarters, you can call the LAN at headquarters and print it there. Not only does this technique save you money, but the text arrives immediately and is better quality than a fax.

■ Dialing In

There are two separate approaches to setting up dial-in services on a LAN: modem remote control and remote node. Each includes its own alternatives. These approaches aren't mutually exclusive, and you can combine them on a single LAN to meet different needs.

Remote Control

The concept of remote control for LAN entry is simple. The caller uses modem remote-control software such as Carbon Copy, CO/Session, or Close-Up to take over a networked PC. The remote-control software is the only software the remote PC runs; there is no LAN software in the calling PC. In effect, the keyboards and screens of the remote and LAN-connected PCs operate in parallel so that keystrokes from the remote PC control the LAN-connected machine and the screen displays of the LAN-connected machine appear on the screen of the remote-control PC. As Figure 9.1 illustrates, the modem link carries screen images to the calling PC and keystrokes to the networked PC. The application programs run on the LAN-connected PC where they have full access to the high-speed network connections and resources. The advantages of this approach include speed and the ability to keep all active files in one place: on the LAN.

People usually begin using remote-control network access by setting up their own office desktop machines to act as remote-control access servers when they are out of the office. Using a desktop PC as a remote-control access server is a simple and direct solution to the problem of how to get remote access, but this informal approach doesn't provide good reliability. For example, power failures cause the office machines to reboot and lose the remote-control program, application programs can cause the remotely controlled PC to freeze, and the active machine with a modem attached provides several ways for someone to breach network security. Additionally, using personal PCs for remote control on an ad hoc basis doesn't provide a standardized method of network access for people who normally work out of the office or in other offices.

Figure 9.1

Under remote-control operation, the calling PC sends keystrokes to the networked PC and receives screen images in return. The calling PC runs only the remote-control software; all application programs run on the networked PC. Some remote-control programs use special techniques to speed the transmission of the dense bitmapped graphics screens created by Windows.

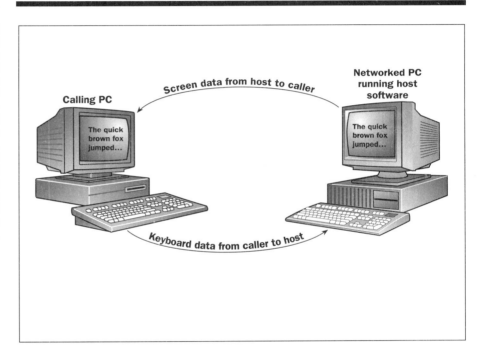

Network administrators and designers work around these drawbacks by setting up dedicated access servers. The most reliable access server is a dedicated PC powered by an uninterrupted power supply and provided with a device, such as Server Technology's Intelligent Power Module, that automatically reboots the PC when the incoming telephone call drops. This type of remote access works on every network regardless of software or media. But as the need for access service grows and more people want to dial into a network at the same time, the network administrator must add more and more PCs. Stacks of PCs dedicated to acting as access servers take up space, so two alternatives for remote control emerged: shared-session access servers and multiple-CPU access servers.

Shared-session access servers, such as Novell's Access Server, use a single CPU, a multiline serial port or modem board, and a multitasking operating system, such as DESQview or Alloy's MultiWare, to provide each caller with a separate session on the network. The advantages of these systems are low cost and the space savings of using only one computer. The drawbacks are slow response time when the system is servicing more than a few callers and incompatibility with some network operating systems and applications. The technique of multiplexing multiple sessions through one network driver and LAN adapter can be incompatible with sophisticated network services.

Multiple-CPU systems provide a much more elegant, although more expensive, alternative. As Figure 9.2 illustrates, specially designed hardware from companies such as J & L Information Systems and Cubix Corporation clusters 4–16 CPUs into a cabinet with a common power supply and a monitoring system that automatically resets each processor as needed. Callers enjoy the fast response time of an individual CPU, while the shared-CPU access server provides reliable operation with good physical and administrative security and excellent compatibility.

Remote-control systems of both types are very popular because of their reliability and because people can keep all files on the LAN, but they have two drawbacks: They require a lot of hardware, and the modem remote-control software slows down under Windows. Modem remote-control programs easily transport the screen presentations generated by character-based video systems, but the dense and fast-changing bitmapped images of a Windows screen take many seconds to traverse the modem link, and the screens of the networked PC appear slowly on the remote PC.

Some modem remote-control software programs, such as Avalan Technology's Remotely Possible Dial, Norton-Lambert's Close-Up, Triton Technologies's CO/Session, and Ocean Isle Software's ReachOut, have been specially configured for Windows. They come with customized Windows screen and keyboard drivers that allow more efficient communications across the modem link—particularly for repetitive tasks.

These programs use special Windows .DLL drivers to intercept and send screen information across the modem connection in compressed form; they don't simply send the contents of the screen display buffer, as older remote-control programs do. In some cases, the programs store specific screens, menu boxes, and other frequently used displays on the calling PC for faster access than sending the same display over the modem line. These products provide tolerably fast screen displays—sort of like running Windows on a 286-based PC—but many people are not satisfied with that level of performance.

Dialing In **151**

Figure 9.2

Products such as the J & L Chatterbox cluster multiple CPUs and LAN adapters into a single cabinet. Because each caller gets the use of a dedicated CPU, these systems have excellent performance. The shared cabinet contains control circuitry to monitor the performance and status of each CPU.

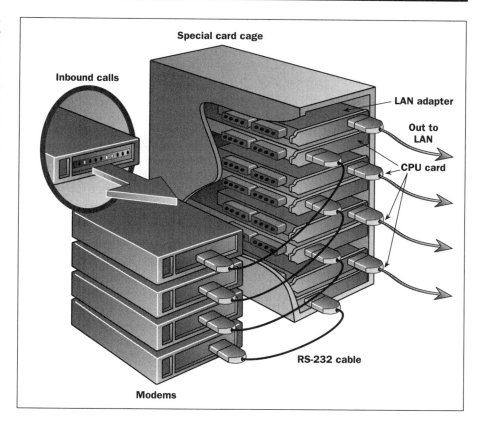

Remote Node

The remote-node technique once was practically abandoned because of its slow throughput. But the migration to Windows, the availability of reasonably priced and powerful laptop and work-at-home computers, and the introduction of reasonably priced modems with 9.6 or 14.4 kilobit-per-second signaling rejuvenated this technique.

Under remote-node operation, illustrated in Figure 9.3, the calling PC loads a full complement of networking software—the full Windows for Workgroups. Under Windows for Workgroups the calling node can be both a remote file server and a remote client. The remote node also must have all necessary application programs. The remote-node PC will probably run under Windows, so it will require 80 megabytes or more of hard-disk storage, at least 4 megabytes of memory, and at least a 386/SX 25 processor.

Figure 9.3

In a remote-node system, each calling PC loads all of its networking and applications programs internally. The portal on the LAN, which simply passes the network packets, can be one PC that can handle many simultaneous callers or a specialized device such as a networked modem.

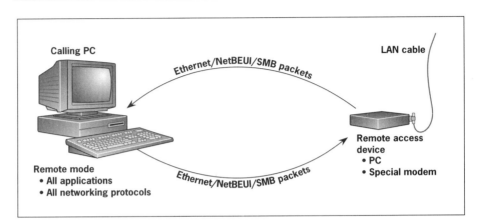

A small program, typically 5–15 kilobytes, supplied by the maker of the access server, routes the input and output of the networking software on the calling PC through the serial port and a modem. All the application programs run on the calling PC instead of running on the networked PC, as they do under the remote-control scheme.

When you call into the network as a remote node, your laptop or work-at-home PC has access to all the shared drives and printers on the network. A small notebook computer can immediately have dozens of DOS disk-drive letters available. The throughput isn't as good as it is for a PC connected directly to the high-speed LAN cable, but it is good enough for all but the most data-intensive applications. Be sure to see our discussion in Chapter 5 concerning the placement of the MSMAIL.MMF file for the most efficient operation of the mail and Schedule+ features of Windows for Workgroups.

Before the development of inexpensive, fast modems and powerful PCs, this remote-node technique wasn't practical because the transfer actions of the networking protocols across the modem link were very inefficient. Faster modems and new software techniques have increased the response time to reasonable levels; however, you must carefully configure the calling PC to avoid pulling .EXE or other executable files across the modem link every time you run them. We discuss this configuration under "Remote-Node Tips" later in this chapter.

Because remote-node products offer good service for people running Windows, we'll look at three different remote-node products from Shiva, DCA, and Microsoft. Shiva's NetModem/E is available in a version specially configured for Windows for Workgroups, and its unique approach offers good throughput and flexibility. DCA's Remote LAN Node (RLN) offers excellent economy and flexibility—particularly for sophisticated network planners who want to mix network protocols from different vendors on the same LAN. Microsoft's LAN Manager Remote Access Service (RAS) offers a traditional approach to remote network access and suffers from the traditional slow response time.

Keep in mind that these products are acting as communications portals on the LAN but not as remotely controlled PCs. In the role of a portal, they don't require the same level of processing power or RAM that a remotely controlled system requires. Overall, the equipment requirements and costs on the LAN side of a remote-node system are less than they are for a remote-control system, but the calling PCs require more power, RAM, and storage capacity.

Shiva NetModem

The Shiva NetModem/E for Windows Workgroups, shown in Figure 9.4, is a high-speed V.32bis modem equipped with a LAN adapter instead of a serial port. It provides telephone connections with a signaling speed of up to 14.4 kilobits per second and it connects directly to the Ethernet cable. You don't need to use a PC as an access server when you use a networked modem. You can use any modem to call into the Shiva NetModem—you don't need another NetModem to place calls—but you'll benefit from using modems with V.32bis signaling and V.42bis data compression and error control when you call the NetModem.

Figure 9.4

The Shiva NetModem/E connects to the network cable and to the telephone line and acts as a portal on the LAN for incoming callers. Special compression techniques provide fast throughput so callers get very good performance.

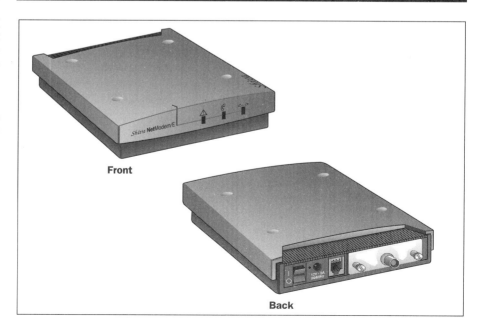

154 Chapter 9: Network Communications

Shiva's programmers tokenize certain repetitive elements of the SMB and NetBEUI protocols to reduce the overhead and improve throughput. This gives you the advantage of using your remote computer as a part of the LAN while still retaining useful throughput.

On the calling PC, a program called SerialLink redirects network traffic through the serial port. SerialLink provides a control panel, shown in Figure 9.5, for setting up the computer's serial port and the modem. If your modem isn't one of those on Shiva's list, you can edit one of the existing modem profiles to meet the need of the modem.

Figure 9.5

This Shiva SerialLink setup menu asks for titles and names that are different from those you use elsewhere in Windows for Workgroups. The Title in this menu is a name you give to the connection—typically a description of the network and its location. The Name is the NetModem/E user name, assigned by the person who set up the NetModem/E on the network, and Password is the NetModem/E password assigned with your user name.

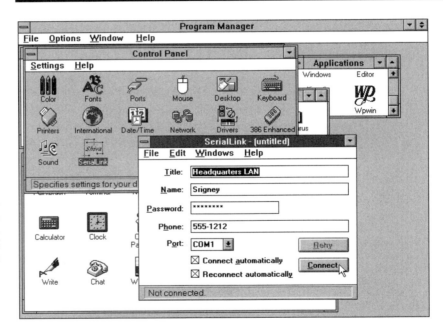

To install the SerialLink driver in a calling PC, you move to the list of network adapter drivers in the Network section of the Windows Control Panel shown in Figure 9.6. From the box listing the network adapter names, you select Unlisted or Updated Network Adapter and click on the Add button. Then the program prompts you for a floppy containing the SerialLink driver. This step only installs the driver; you still must run Shiva's setup program.

You can have LAN adapter cards in the PC you use to make the call to the Shiva modem. The Shiva SerialLink drivers will coexist with the other LAN card drivers and you'll see the resources of both the local network attached to the LAN adapter and the remote network connected through the serial port and modem. Be careful about selecting IRQs for these other adapters that could conflict with the IRQ 3 or 4 used by the PC's serial ports, because you'll be using at least one of those ports for the modem.

Figure 9.6

After callers choose the Unlisted or Updated Network Adapter option from the Network section of the Windows Control Panel and insert a floppy with the appropriate driver, their network packets are delivered to a modem connected to the appropriate serial port.

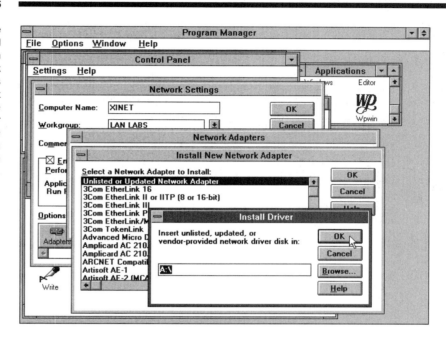

DCA Remote LAN Node

Another product that provides efficient remote client operation for any network is the Remote LAN Node (RLN) from DCA. Unlike the Shiva Net-Modem, the RLN system will work with any network operating system that has drivers for either the Clarkson Packet Driver or the Microsoft/IBM NDIS interface.

RLN is a software product that runs on any networked PC. This PC acts as an access server for remote clients. The server software can theoretically handle as many as 16 remote connections, so you'll want to run it on a PC with at least an 80386SX processor running at 20 megahertz. DCA bundles a DigiBoard multiport RS-232 board with microprocessor augmentation to relieve the PC's CPU of many I/O tasks so you get good performance at the network portal. The selection of modems you use with RLN is up to you, but you should not use anything less than V.32bis modems with 14.4 kilobit-per-second signaling and V.42bis data compression and error control.

On the calling PC, you use software provided by DCA to route the network packets to the serial port. The RLN client software isn't as well integrated into Windows for Workgroups as the Shiva software. You must run separate programs to use RLN, while the NetModem's services appear as menu choices in the File Manager pull-down menus.

Shiva and DCA use several different techniques to speed the transmission of data across the modem link. Shiva uses V.42bis compression in its software to improve throughput, and it supports Novell's Large Internet Exchange Packet that streams data across the link more efficiently.

DCA's RLN uses Internet's Point-to-Point Protocol (PPP). PPP includes tokenizing and compression techniques that work very well on network packets. These techniques include Tinygram Compression, which strips the trailing zeros from any minimum-size packet, Header Compression, which reduces redundant and unnecessary data from a header, and Protocol Length Compression, which handles the problems of packets broken up for transmission. PPP doesn't do error handling, so you still need to use a modem with V.42 or MNP services to ensure the integrity of the data going over the line. It is important to note that DCA's RLN works with practically any network operating system and, in fact, the RLN access server will simultaneously host calling nodes using different network operating systems, such as Windows for Workgroups and NetWare.

LAN Manager Remote Access Service

Microsoft's LAN Manager Remote Access Service (RAS) comes in two flavors: one for DOS PCs and one for those running Windows. Either package contains only software, allows as many as 16 remote nodes to call in at once, and costs $1,995.

Microsoft's RAS communications software runs on a LAN Manager server over the multitasking OS/2 or Windows NT operating systems. The software identifies callers and provides a remote-node connection into the network.

You can use RAS in a PC and connect modems to the PC's internal serial ports, but we suggest using a multiport adapter board with built-in buffering and processing, such as those available from Hayes and DigiBoard. These boards have a smoother and less disruptive interface with the PC's CPU and memory system than the internal ports. Additionally, DigiBoard sells boards that can provide a dozen simultaneous connections while avoiding the problems of finding interrupt addresses.

We mention RAS because it is Microsoft's product and you'll probably hear about it as an alternative for remote access into Windows for Workgroups networks. However, RAS doesn't employ the compression techniques used by RLN or the Shiva modem, so it has much slower throughput.

Remote-Node Tips

Your success with remote-node access systems depends on how well you configure your remote PC for operation. The basic rules for happiness are as follows: Pull as little as possible across the telephone line and never pull an .EXE, .INI, or .COM file from the network. Under NetWare, utilities such as LOGIN, MAP, CAPTURE, USERLIST, WHOAMI, SYSCON, and FILER, and other programs that the caller might use should be loaded on the remote PC.

Under remote-node operation, Windows programs run as fast as the calling PC allows, you don't need a lot of processing power in the access server, and you can still keep the data files on the LAN. However, it can take longer to load those data files, you need more processing power in the calling PC, and you must carefully configure the calling PC.

Deciding Factors

Which type of remote-access system is best for your Windows for Workgroups installation? Perhaps both! The answer depends completely on what the people calling into the network want to do once they make the connection and on the capability of the computers they are using to make the call. Here are some factors to consider when making your decision:

- Remote-control systems are more useful than remote-node systems for network administrators and troubleshooters calling into the LAN. An administrator can access a wide variety of utilities that monitor all the traffic and functions of the network using a remotely controlled networked PC. It is too difficult for a remote-node system to pull these high volumes of data over a modem link.

- Remote-node systems are better for remote printing. You can move large print jobs containing graphic images to highly capable networked printers through the remote-node link more easily than you can create them on a remotely controlled PC or send them over the remote-control modem link.

- Remote-control systems are better for people who want to keep their working and archive files in one place. For example, using e-mail packages on a remote-node system can result in two sets of folders containing electronic messages, one on the remote-node PC and one on the office PC.

- Remote-node systems are better for people who have powerful PCs at home or on the road. PCs operating as remote nodes must hold many programs and run modern applications.

- Remote-control systems with customized software, such as Ocean Isle's Remote Control for Windows, can give good throughput for many Windows applications, particularly those that use standard menus and figures and not customized bitmaps. Remote-control systems are better for people who infrequently use standard Windows applications.

- Remote-node systems always offer fast program execution, but it might take many seconds to access a file. They are better for people who rely heavily on Windows programs—particularly people who use graphics such as diagrams or presentation materials.

- Because of their size and reasonable cost, networked modems make it easy to incrementally add more devices as you need more capacity.

- The DCA RLN requires an entire PC to act as a remote-node access server, but it is more flexible than a networked modem because it will work with a variety of network operating systems and applications. The RLN system can grow from 2 to 16 remote nodes within the same dedicated PC.

■ Dialing Out

A local area network also provides a good way to share high-speed modems for dial-out services. At first glance, it may not seem to make economic sense to share modems, because even 14.4 kilobit-per-second modems now carry reasonable price tags. However, the savings you get from sharing isn't in modem equipment costs, it is in telephone lines and installation services. Business telephone lines can cost $70 to $100 per month. In addition, many office telephone systems are not designed to accept modems. In some buildings, running the phone wires presents a problem. So if you already have an installed LAN, you can add a modem server to avoid other costs.

A modem server makes a group of modems—as few as 1 or 2 or as many as 16 or 24—available to the client workstations on a first-come, first-served basis. People at the client stations use software able to communicate across the network, such as DCA's CrossTalk Mk.4, to establish a dedicated connection to a modem in the modem pool. The modem server gives the PC winning its services its full attention for as long as the call lasts—a condition called a *virtual circuit*.

Sharing networked modems is tricky because communications programs are designed to write to serial-port hardware instead of to a DOS function call that is easily redirected to the LAN. If you want a communications program to address a modem across a LAN, you basically have two alternatives: change the hardware or change the software.

Microsoft included a function call, interrupt 14, in DOS for serial communications. Because it was slow, people writing communications programs bypassed DOS and addressed the serial ports directly. If an application talks directly to the hardware, the network redirector—which can grab only requests made to DOS—can't divert the requests out through the LAN adapter to a communications server.

Modem server products depend on either interrupt 14 or a similar network service called the Network Asynchronous Server Interface (NASI), developed by Novell. NASI requires the communications software to use interrupt 6BH to ask for network services. In our recent review of 23 general-purpose communications programs, 14 programs offered drivers for both interrupt 14 and NASI, and 5 more offered only interrupt 14 drivers. However, you often must upgrade to the latest version of the program to use the network drivers.

Although you can find a general-purpose communications package you'll be happy with, it's unlikely that a special program designed to access a remote database or an on-line service can use interrupt 14 or NASI; Lotus Express for MCI Mail is one example of a special program without network support. So specialized and vertical applications often cannot take advantage of networked modems.

Besides the right kind of communications software, any PC that uses shared networked modems must run a special redirector program for interrupt 14 or NASI. Typically you load a TSR of about 20 kilobytes, provided by the vendor of the communications server, that moves the data between the communications software and the network driver. During the setup, you tell the redirector how to use available shared modems on a first-come, first-served basis.

You can use the networked modems to control access to telephone services. You might, for example, have long-distance lines with unlimited dialing capabilities and specify in the interrupt 14 or NASI redirector a pool of networked modems connected to them as COM3. Another group of modems, perhaps attached to private lines going only to different operating locations in your organization, could be assigned to COM4. You can password-protect each networked modem to limit access. Anyone wanting to use a shared modem runs communications software with interrupt 14 or NASI service, selecting the appropriate communications port.

The redirector posts a notice if no modem is available; otherwise, the operation proceeds normally.

Several companies, including US Robotics, MultiTech, and Cross Communications Company, offer a variety of dial-out products that use interrupt 14 or NASI. These range from a $495 program, Cross+Connect Modem Share, that allows any networked PC to make its attached modem available to other networked PCs, to eight-port dedicated modem asynchronous communications servers with price tags of nearly $3,000.

But other companies, including J & L Information Systems and D-Link Systems, sell hardware redirectors that you insert into the expansion bus of any PC needing shared modem services. Because these redirectors emulate a communications port, they'll work with any communications software. However, they work only with proprietary communications servers and don't offer a way to use standard programs with the networked modems in this review.

- *Installing the Workgroup Connection*
- *Using the Workgroup Connection*
- *Using the NET Command-Line Interface*

CHAPTER

10

The Workgroup Connection

W<small>HILE MUCH OF THE COMPUTER COMMUNITY'S ATTENTION IS</small> focused on Windows, there are millions of older XT- and AT-class machines still in use every day. These machines lack the horsepower required to run Windows, but they are still serviceable, practical DOS workhorses. In addition, there are millions of DOS users who prefer the familiar DOS prompt to the graphical interface of Windows.

The Microsoft Workgroup Connection is a collection of DOS programs that allows DOS PCs to connect to shared disks and printers on Windows for Workgroups and LAN Manager servers. The Workgroup Connection also includes a DOS version of the Microsoft Mail program, which allows DOS users to exchange mail messages with Windows for Workgroups users.

The Workgroup Connection can run on virtually any MS-DOS–based PC, as long as the PC is running DOS version 3.3 or later. The Workgroup Connection requires very little in terms of memory, disk space, and processing power, and can run on older 8088- and 8086-based PCs that cannot run Windows.

The Workgroup Connection has two major shortcomings when compared to Windows for Workgroups. First, the Workgroup Connection is a client-only product. Workgroup Connection machines cannot provide shared resources for others to use. Second, Workgroup Connection clients can connect to LAN Manager servers, but not to Novell NetWare servers. If your company has a NetWare LAN, you'll have to choose between connecting to the Windows for Workgroups network or to the NetWare LAN; you can't connect to both at once.

■ Installing the Workgroup Connection

Because the Workgroup Connection and Windows for Workgroups share many of the same files, you shouldn't install the Workgroup Connection on a PC that already has Windows for Workgroups. The Workgroup Connection SETUP program changes the CONFIG.SYS file in ways that may conflict with your Windows for Workgroups installation. The Windows for Workgroups package includes all the Workgroup Connection software, except for the DOS version of the Mail program. The Workgroup Connection software was installed in your C:\WINDOWS directory when you installed Windows for Workgroups. If you have Windows for Workgroups installed on your PC, you can use all the features of the Workgroup Connection except for the DOS-based electronic mail features. For the remainder of this section, we'll assume that you're installing the Workgroup Connection on a DOS PC without Windows for Workgroups.

Before you install the Workgroup Connection software, you must install a supported network adapter board in your PC. See Chapter 3 for details on hardware installation. Also, make backup copies of your CONFIG.SYS and AUTOEXEC.BAT files. The Workgroup Connection SETUP program changes your CONFIG.SYS and AUTOEXEC.BAT files without asking permission. If the Workgroup Connection isn't installed correctly on the first try, you may need to restore your original CONFIG.SYS and AUTOEXEC.BAT files.

Installing the Workgroup Connection   165

To begin the software installation process, place the Workgroup Connection diskette in a floppy drive and run the SETUP program from the floppy. The SETUP program signs on and asks you to specify a directory in which to install the Workgroup Connection Files. The default directory is C:\DOS, but you may specify a different directory. In our examples, we'll place the Workgroup Connection files in C:\DOS\WC.

After you specify the installation directory, the SETUP program examines your PC's hardware and software to determine what type of network card you have and to determine whether Microsoft LAN Manager is already installed. Although this process takes only a few seconds on 80386 and 80486 machines, there's a remarkable amount of behind-the-scenes detective work going on. The SETUP program carefully examines your PC's system BIOS, peripheral ROMs, I/O address space, and installed device drivers (Figure 10.1). SETUP compares this information with a built-in database to determine the exact type of network card installed in your PC as well as the optimal IRQ and I/O address settings for the card. In our testing, the SETUP program correctly determined our LAN adapter setup ten times out of ten.

Figure 10.1

SETUP displays this message while it examines your system's existing hardware and software. Although the message says that the process may take a few minutes, it usually takes only a few seconds.

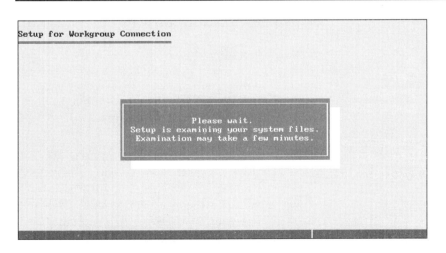

After SETUP determines your PC's configuration information, the program asks you to provide a name for your computer. The computer name may be up to 15 characters long and must be unique; no other machine may have the same name. After you supply a computer name, the SETUP program asks you to provide a user name. Like Windows for Workgroups user names, this user name identifies you to other users on the network. The user name may be up to 20 characters long. Finally, SETUP asks you to enter your workgroup name.

After you enter the workgroup name, SETUP displays a list of options like the one shown in Figure 10.2. In most cases, the default settings provided by SETUP are correct, and you can simply press Enter to complete the installation.

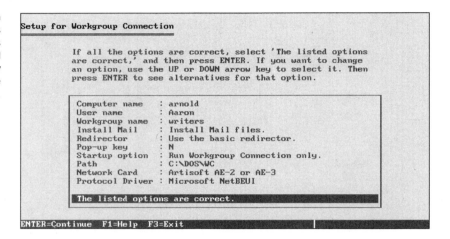

Figure 10.2

The SETUP program displays this options screen before it begins copying files to your hard disk. You can change any of the options before the installation begins.

NOTE. *If you have previously installed LAN Manager or Windows for Workgroups on your PC, the SETUP program will pick up the installation directory, machine name, user name, and workgroup name from your PROTOCOL.INI file. If this happens, do* not *install the Workgroup Connection files in the same directory as your LAN Manager or Windows for Workgroups files.*

If you want to change any of the options, use the Up Arrow and Down Arrow keys to highlight the desired entry and press Enter. Table 7.1 lists all the options and explains the possible settings for each option.

When you're satisfied with the options screen, press Enter to save the options. SETUP copies the necessary files from the floppy to your hard disk. When the installation is complete, SETUP prompts you to press Enter to reboot the system or press F3 to exit to DOS. When you reboot your system, the Workgroup Connection software loads automatically from AUTOEXEC.BAT.

If you want to change your network options later, switch to the directory where you installed the Workgroup Connection software and run SETUP again. It is not necessary to run SETUP from the original floppy.

NOTE. *On 80386 and 80486 machines with an extended memory manager program, the Workgroup Connection software automatically loads into high memory if enough high memory is available.*

Table 10.1

The Workgroup Connection Installation Options

OPTION	POSSIBLE SETTINGS
Computer Name	Any valid computer name up to 15 characters.
User Name	Any valid user name up to 20 characters.
Workgroup Name	Any valid workgroup name.
Install Mail	• Install Mail program files (default). • Do not install Mail program files.
Redirector	Use basic (default) or full redirector. The full redirector supports advanced network functions including named pipes but uses significantly more memory. If your PC has an 8088 or 8086 CPU, you cannot use the full redirector.
Pop-Up Key	Any Alt key combination from Alt+A to Alt+Z. The default setting is Alt+N.
Startup Option	• Run Workgroup Connection only. • Run Workgroup Connection and log on (default setting). • Run Workgroup Connection, log on, and load pop-up menu. • Do not run Workgroup Connection.
Path	Any valid DOS path name (must be on boot drive).
Network Card	Determined automatically by SETUP. If SETUP selects the wrong driver for your card, press Enter and select your card from the list of available drivers.
Protocol Driver	Windows for Workgroups and Workgroup Connection normally use the default protocol: Microsoft NetBEUI. If your network uses a different protocol, you'll need a protocol driver disk from your LAN vendor.

■ Using the Workgroup Connection

The Workgroup Connection has two user interfaces, both of which are available through the same program: NET.EXE. Using this program you can control the Workgroup Connection through a series of on-screen menus or directly from the DOS command line. If you start NET with no options, NET will use the menu interface. If you give NET a complete command, such as

```
NET USE F: \\MARVIN\MAIN
```

then NET will carry out your command and return to DOS. (In our sample command, we told NET to connect logical drive F: to the shared disk MAIN on the server MARVIN.) The command-line options are especially useful in batch files, because they allow you to perform a series of NET commands in sequence. We'll examine the NET command-line options in detail in the upcoming sections.

The first time you run NET after installing the Workgroup Connection, you'll be prompted to enter a user name and password that identify you to the network. NET stores your user name and password information in an encrypted file on the hard disk. The next time you start your PC and run NET, you'll be prompted to enter your password.

The NET Pop-Up Menu

After you enter your user name and password, you'll see the NET pop-up menu. This one simple menu, shown in Figure 10.3, lets you perform these functions:

- Connect and disconnect network disks
- Connect and disconnect network printers
- Monitor network print jobs
- Pause, resume, and delete pending print jobs

Figure 10.3

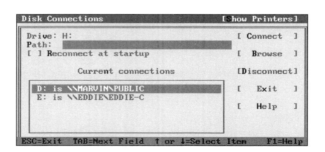

The NET pop-up menus let you connect and disconnect network disks and printers and manage print jobs. This picture shows the Disk Connections menu.

The NET pop-up menu has two parts: the Disk Connections menu and the Printer Connections menu. Pressing the Alt+S key from one menu screen switches to the other. Figure 10.3 shows the Disk Connections menu; the Printer Connections menu is very similar in appearance.

Loading NET as a TSR Program

In normal operation, the NET menu appears when you start NET and then disappears when you're finished with NET. If you want to change your network drive and printer settings, you must exit your application program and start NET again. If you wish, you can load NET as a terminate-and-stay-resident (TSR) program. In this mode, NET is always ready to use, and you can switch to it by pressing your NET pop-up key combination—usually Alt+N. The downside is that the NET pop-up TSR uses about 32 kilobytes of DOS memory.

To load NET as a TSR program, type NET START POP from the DOS prompt. Here is what will happen:

```
C:\> NET START POP
Pop-up for Workgroup Connection loaded into memory.
Use Alt+N to activate.
The command completed successfully.
```

Once you've loaded the NET TSR, press the pop-up key to pop up the NET menu. Note that NET will not pop up if the system display is running in graphics mode. Some word processors (notably Microsoft Word 5.5) and most CAD programs run in graphics mode, so the NET pop-up menu will not be available from these programs.

If you want to remove the pop-up TSR from memory, type NET STOP POP from the DOS prompt. Note that you can't unload the NET TSR if you load any other TSR programs after NET.

Connecting and Disconnecting Network Disks

You use the Disk Connections screen to connect and disconnect network disks. As you can see from Figure 10.3, the lower part of the Disk Connections screen displays a list of your current network disk connections. To connect to a network disk from a Workgroup Connection PC, follow these steps:

1. Type NET at the DOS command line or press the pop-up key combination if the NET pop-up menu is loaded. NET automatically displays the next available drive letter in the Drive setting box.

2. If you want to use the displayed letter, go to the next step. To change the drive letter, press Alt+V and then type the letter of the drive you want to use.

3. If you know the exact pathname (for example, \\MARVIN\MAIN) of the shared disk, you can type it in the Path box, press Alt+C to connect the disk, and skip to step 6.

4. If you don't know the exact path name, press Alt+B to browse through the available network disks.

5. Select a server with the Up Arrow and Down Arrow keys and then use the Tab key to select the Shared Directories window. Select a shared disk with the Up Arrow and Down Arrow keys and press Enter.

6. If the shared disk has a password, enter it when asked. The main Disk Connections screen reappears, and your new drive connection should appear in the Current Connections list.

7. If you want to automatically reconnect to the network disks the next time you start your PC, press Alt+R to check the Reconnect at Startup check box.

8. Press Alt+X to exit the Disk Connections menu.

To disconnect from a network disk, follow these steps:

1. Start NET from the DOS command line or press the pop-up key combination.

2. Press Alt+N to move the cursor to the Current Connections display. Use the Up Arrow and Down Arrow keys to select the drive to disconnect.

3. Press Alt+D to disconnect from the network drive.

4. Press Alt+X to exit the Disk Connections menu.

Connecting and Disconnecting Network Printers

MS-DOS supports three printer ports, named LPT1 through LPT3. The Workgroup Connection software allows you to connect any of the three printer ports to any network printer. For example, you can connect port LPT2 to an HP LaserJet printer on one server and LPT3 to a PostScript printer on another server. You control these printer assignments through the Printer Connections screen.

The Printer Connections screen (Figure 10.4) looks like the Disk Network Connections screen and works in much the same way. When you start the NET pop-up menu, the NET program presents the Disk Connections display. To see the Printer Connections display, press Alt+S from the Disk Connections display. Conversely, pressing Alt+S from the Printer Connections display returns you to the Disk Connections display.

To connect a network printer from a Workgroup Connection PC, follow these steps:

1. Type NET at the DOS command line, or press the pop-up key combination if the NET pop-up menu is loaded. NET displays the Disk Connections screen.

Figure 10.4

The Printer Connections screen allows you to connect, disconnect, and view network printers.

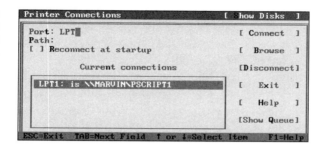

2. Press Alt+S to switch the display to the Printer Connections screen. Any existing printer connections will appear in the Current Connections display, and the cursor will be on the Port field.

3. Type the port number (1 to 3) to use for your network printer.

4. If you know the full path name (for example, \\MARVIN\LASER) of the printer you want to use, press Alt+P, type the name of the printer in the Path box, and press Alt+C to connect the printer.

5. If you want to automatically reconnect to this printer the next time you start Workgroup Connection, press Alt+R to check the Reconnect at Startup check box.

6. If you don't know the name of the printer you want to use, press Alt+B to browse the shared printers list. Use the Up Arrow and Down Arrow keys to select a server from the list in the top portion of the display.

7. Press the Tab key to move the cursor to the lower window, and select a printer with the Up Arrow and Down Arrow keys.

8. When you've selected the printer, press Enter to connect it.

9. Press Alt+X or Esc to exit the Printer Connections menu.

To disconnect a network printer from a Workgroup Connection PC, follow these steps:

1. Type NET at the DOS command line or press the pop-up key combination if the NET pop-up menu is loaded. NET displays the Disk Connections screen.

2. Press Alt+S to switch the display to the Printer Connections screen. Your printer connections will appear in the Current Connections display, and the cursor will be on the Port field.

3. Type the port number (1 to 3) you want to disconnect.

4. Press Alt+D to disconnect the printer. The printer disappears from the Current Connections list.

5. Press Alt+X or Esc to exit the Printer Connections screen.

Checking Print Jobs

Network software must deal with several users trying to use the same printer at once. LAN Manager and Windows for Workgroups accomplish this through the use of *print queues*. A print queue is a holding area for print jobs on their way to the printer. Each shared printer has a print queue. As jobs are printed by users, the server places them in the appropriate queue. This process (also known as *spooling*) allows an application program running on a client PC user to print very quickly, because the software does not have to wait for the printer. The print data flows from your PC to the server at a very high speed. Once your print job is sent to the server, your PC is free for other work.

When users (or their application programs) signal that they are finished printing, the server passes the queued print job on to the printer. This may take some time, depending on the number of jobs ahead of yours. Print jobs are normally handled on a first-come, first-served basis.

The Workgroup Connection Print Queue screen (Figure 10.5) provides a way for you to view and control the jobs in a print queue. To see the Print Queue screen, press Alt+Q from the Printer Connections screen. In Figure 10.5, our sample PC is attached to two network printers. The printer \\MARVIN\PSCRIPT1 has five print jobs waiting; printer \\EDDIE\HPDESKJET has none.

Figure 10.5

The Print Queue screen provides a way for you to view and manipulate the jobs in a printer queue.

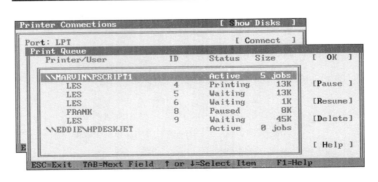

You can use the Print Queue screen to pause, resume, or delete your own print jobs. You cannot change the status of another user's print jobs.

To pause, resume, or delete a print job, follow these steps:

1. Type NET at the DOS command line or press the pop-up key combination if the NET pop-up menu is loaded. NET displays the Disk Connections screen.
2. Press Alt+S to switch to the Printer Connections screen.
3. Press Alt+Q to see the Print Queue screen.
4. Select the desired print job with the Up Arrow and Down Arrow keys.
5. Press Alt+P to pause the print job, Alt+R to resume a paused print job, or Alt+D to delete a job.
6. Press Esc to exit the Print Queue screen.

■ Using the NET Command-Line Interface

So far, we've shown you how to run Workgroup Connection from the NET pop-up menu Disk Connections and Printer Connections screens. The NET.EXE program can also accept commands directly from the DOS command line. In the upcoming sections, we'll discuss the NET DOS command-line commands.

The Command-Line Interface

The Workgroup Connection network manager program (NET.EXE) can accept direct commands from the DOS command line or from a DOS batch file. The command-line interface provides an extra degree of flexibility and speeds up network operations. For example, it takes five steps to connect a network disk with the menu system:

1. Start the NET.EXE program.
2. Enter your user name and password if you aren't already logged in.
3. Select the drive letter to use for the network drive.
4. Select a server from the list of servers.
5. Select a network disk to use.

To perform the same steps with the NET.EXE command line, you'd enter the command

```
NET USE D: \\MARVIN\C-DRIVE
```

This command redirects drive D to the shared disk C-DRIVE on the server MARVIN. This one command line replaces the five steps it takes to use the menu system.

Another advantage of the command-line interface is that you can use the NET.EXE command lines to create batch files. Batch files are files that contain DOS commands; since any program name is a DOS command, you can use a batch file to load and run virtually any program on your system.

Batch-file commands are entered one command per line. You can use any plain text editor to create batch files; the EDIT.EXE text editor supplied with DOS 5.0 is ideal. A DOS batch file must have the file type .BAT.

When you run a batch file, DOS reads the command lines from the batch file one at a time and passes each command line to the DOS command processor. By combining the appropriate NET commands in a DOS batch file, you can log in, attach printers, and connect to network disk drives by typing a single command.

The example below shows a batch file named LOGIN.BAT. This batch file starts the redirector, attaches two network drives and a printer, and shows the status of the user's network connection:

```
@REM LOGIN.BAT - Log in and attach net drives and printer
@echo off
net start workstation
net use lpt1 \\alr486\HPDESKJET
net use F: \\MARVIN\c-drive
net use G: \\EDDIE\d-drive
net use
```

There are some operations that can only be performed from the NET command line. In the following sections, we'll explain each of the NET command-line options.

NET.EXE Command-Line Options

This section lists each of the NET command-line options in alphabetical order. Where appropriate, we'll show you a sample usage. Items shown in brackets [ ] are optional. Items shown in parentheses ( ) are required. Items in curly braces { } must be one of the options specified. All other items must be entered in the order shown.

NET CONFIG

Syntax NET CONFIG

Usage NET CONFIG displays your current network configuration information, including your workgroup name, computer name, user name, and network software versions.

Example NET CONFIG

NET HELP

Syntax   NET HELP

NET HELP (command)

NET HELP (error number)

Usage   The NET HELP command provides usage information for each NET command. Type NET HELP to see a brief summary of all the NET commands. For help with a specific command, type NET HELP *command*, where *command* is the command you need help with.

Occasionally, the Workgroup Connection may display an error message when you enter a command. For a complete explanation of the error, type NET HELP *error*, where *error* is the error number.

Examples   NET HELP USE

NET HELP 53

NET LOGOFF

Syntax   NET LOGOFF [/Y]

Usage   The NET LOGOFF command logs you off the network and disconnects any shared resources attached to your PC. If you are attached to a shared disk or printer, NET will warn you before completing the logoff request. You can override the warning message with the /Y option.

Examples   NET LOGOFF

NET LOGOFF /Y

NET LOGON

Syntax   NET LOGON [username [password]] /Y

Usage   The NET LOGON command logs you on to the network and reconnects any permanent connections you may have defined. NET needs to know your user name and password before it can connect you to the network. If you don't provide a user name, you'll be prompted to enter your user name and password. If you provide a user name but no password, you'll be prompted to enter the password.

Chapter 10: The Workgroup Connection

The /Y option instructs NET to log you on even though your PC may already be logged on under another name. The /Y option has the same effect as NET LOGOFF /Y followed by a NET LOGON command.

Examples

```
NET LOGON
NET LOGON DANQ POTATOE /Y
```

NET PASSWORD

Syntax

```
NET PASSWORD [oldpassword newpassword]
NET PASSWORD [\\server][user [oldpw [newpw]]]
NET PASSWORD [/domain:name][user [oldpw [newpw]]]
```

Usage

The NET PASSWORD command changes your password on a Workgroup Connection–Windows for Workgroups network or on a LAN Manager network. The first syntax shown above is for use on Workgroup Connection–Windows for Workgroups networks. You may enter the old and new passwords on the command line; if you don't, the NET program will prompt you to enter them.

The second and third command lines are for use on LAN Manager networks. If you specify a server name, NET will change your password on the specified server. If you specify a domain name, NET will change your password for the specified domain.

Examples

```
NET PASSWORD potatoe tomatoe
NET PASSWORD \\MARVIN Ross maybeiam maybeimnot
NET PASSWORD /DOMAIN:Writers Judy
```

NET PRINT

Syntax

```
NET PRINT (server) [job#]
NET PRINT (port) [job#]
```

Options

```
/PAUSE
/RESUME
/DELETE
```

Using the NET Command-Line Interface   **177**

Usage NET PRINT displays and modifies print queues. You can specify the print queue to examine by providing either the server name or the printer port name.

Used with no options, NET PRINT displays the contents of the specified print queue along with a job number for each queue entry. Once you know the job number for a specific job, you can use the /PAUSE, /RESUME, or /DELETE option to pause, resume, or delete a specific print job.

Examples
```
NET PRINT \\MARVIN
NET PRINT LPT1
NET PRINT LPT1 192 /DELETE
```

NET START

Syntax
```
NET START
NET START POPUP
NET START BASIC
NET START FULL
```

Options
```
/LIST
/YES
```

Usage NET START loads the Workgroup Connection redirector software into memory and optionally starts certain network services. In most cases, you can simply type NET START to load and start the Workgroup Connection.

NET START BASIC starts the basic workstation redirector (the default condition), while NET START FULL starts the full redirector. Use the full redirector only if you need access to LAN Manager named pipes or other extended services on a LAN Manager server; otherwise, use the smaller basic redirector.

NET START POPUP starts the redirector program and loads the optional pop-up network interface. You can access the pop-up menu from any DOS program by pressing the pop-up key combination.

178 Chapter 10: The Workgroup Connection

NET START /LIST displays your current redirector settings. The /Y option tells NET to perform the NET START command without displaying any warning messages.

Examples   `NET START BASIC`

                   `NET START POPUP`

                   `NET START /LIST`

NET STOP

Syntax   `NET STOP`

              `NET STOP POPUP`

              `NET STOP BASIC`

              `NET STOP FULL`

Options   `/Y`

Usage   NET STOP is the opposite of NET START; you use NET STOP to stop the redirector software and unload it from memory. If you are connected to any shared resources, the NET program will prompt you with a warning message before it disconnects them. You can override the warning message with the /Y option; NET STOP /Y will cause the NET program to immediately disconnect any shared resources.

Examples   `NET STOP BASIC`

                   `NET STOP /Y`

NET TIME

Syntax   `NET TIME \\server`

              `NET TIME /WORKGROUP:groupname`

Options   `/SET`

              `/Y`

Usage   You can use NET TIME to synchronize your computer's clock with the shared clock service on a LAN Manager time server. *server* specifies the name of the server to get the time from; WORKGROUP:*groupname* specifies that you want to use the clock on a server in a different workgroup. You must use the /SET option to actually change your PC's clock; without the /SET option, NET TIME will only display the time received from the time server. The /Y option tells NET to change your PC's time without displaying a warning message.

Examples   `NET TIME \\MARVIN`

                `NET TIME /WORKGROUP:Writers /Y`

NET USE

Syntax   `NET USE [drive:] [\\server\path [password]`

                `NET USE [port:] [\\server\queue [password]`

                `NET USE`

Options   `/PERSISTENT:{YES | NO | LIST | SAVE | CLEAR} / SAVEPW:NO`

                `/YES`

                `/DELETE`

Usage   One of the key NET commands, NET USE redirects a local drive or printer port to a shared network device. There are three forms of this command: one each for network drives and printers and one to display your current connections.

The first form of the NET USE command connects a local drive letter specified by *drive*: to a network directory contained in *path* on *server*. If you specify an asterisk (*) as the drive letter, NET will use the next available drive letter.

The second form of NET USE connects the local printer port specified by *port* to the printer queue named *queue* on *server*.

The /DELETE option causes NET to disconnect the specified drive or printer. For example, the command

NET USE D: /DELETE

causes NET to disconnect the network disk connected to drive D. If you specify an asterisk (*) as the drive letter, NET will disconnect all network disks. Similarly,

NET USE LPT1: /DELETE

will disconnect the network printer from port LPT1.

The /PERSISTENT option specifies which connections should be automatically reconnected (persistent) the next time you log on to the network. There are five settings for the /PERSISTENT option:

- YES indicates that the connection you are making and any additional connections should be persistent.
- NO indicates that the connection you are making and any additional connections should not be persistent.
- SAVE copies all your existing connections to the persistent-connections list.
- LIST displays your existing persistent connections.
- CLEAR removes all your persistent connections from the persistent-connections list.

When you connect to a password-protected shared resource, the Workgroup Connection normally saves the resource password in your password-list file. The option /SAVEPW:NO indicates that the resource password should not be added to the password-list file.

The command NET USE by itself displays a list of all shared resources currently in use by your workstation.

Examples

NET USE G: \\MARVIN\MAIN
NET USE * \\MARVIN\C-DRIVE
NET USE LPT1: \\EDDIE\HPLASER
NET USE LPT1: /DELETE

NET VER

Syntax   NET VER

Usage   NET VER displays the type (basic or full) and version of the redirector software on your PC.

NET VIEW

Syntax   NET VIEW [\\server]

              NET VIEW [/WORKGROUP:groupname]

              NET VIEW

Usage   NET VIEW displays the shared resources available on a specific server and also displays a list of servers available in a workgroup.

- *The Windows for Workgroups Initialization Files*
- *Monitoring and Managing Network Activity*
- *Managing Print Queues*
- *Defining Additional Printer Ports*
- *Restricting Shared Resources*
- *Inhibiting the Startup Group*
- *Managing Persistent Network Connections*

- *Locking Up the Program Manager*
- *LAN Manager Visibility*

CHAPTER

11

Fine-Tuning Windows for Workgroups

Windows for Workgroups provides a large number of customization options. In the upcoming sections, we'll take a look at some of these options and offer some tips for customizing and optimizing Windows for Workgroups. There are literally thousands of customization options available; we'll concentrate on the network-related ones.

For more general information about customization, see the *Windows for Workgroups User's Guide* (included with Windows for Workgroups); the *Windows for Workgroups Resource Kit* (available directly from Microsoft); and *PC Magazine Guide to Windows 3.1,* by Gus Venditto (published by Ziff-Davis Press).

■ The Windows for Workgroups Initialization Files

When you install Windows for Workgroups, the SETUP program analyzes your system and creates several *initialization files.* These files describe your hardware, software, and user preferences to Windows. When you start Windows for Workgroups, it reads these files to determine how to configure Windows for your system and your personal preferences.

When you use Windows for Workgroups, you may change certain program settings and options from program menus; these changes are usually stored in an initialization file so that Windows for Workgroups will remember your changes the next time you start it. In most cases, you can run Windows for Workgroups without ever having to concern yourself with these files. Some options, however, can be changed only by editing the associated initialization file.

The initialization information is contained in nine files. Some application programs create their own initialization files, and other programs add their own settings to the WIN.INI file. Table 11.1 explains the purpose of each of the standard initialization files.

Before we dig into the particulars, there are a few things you need to know about the .INI files. You must edit the .INI files with a text editor capable of editing "plain text," or ASCII, files. The Windows Notepad program and the DOS 5 EDIT.EXE program both edit plain text files. You can also use SYSEDIT.EXE, the Windows System Configuration Editor program included with Windows for Workgroups, to edit SYSTEM.INI, WIN.INI, CONFIG.SYS, and AUTOEXEC.BAT all at the same time. The System Configuration Editor is installed in your WINDOWS\SYSTEM directory by the Windows SETUP program. When you run SYSEDIT, the program automatically opens your AUTOEXEC.BAT, CONFIG.SYS, WIN.INI, and SYSTEM.INI files and displays them in four windows. Figure 11.1 shows the SYSEDIT program being used to edit the configuration files.

Note that your favorite word processor may or may not be able to edit plain text files. Many word processing programs place formatting information into files, and this formatting information will render the file useless to Windows.

Table 11.1

The Standard Initialization Files

FILE NAME	CONTAINS
CONTROL.INI	Colors, patterns, wallpaper file name, installable driver names, printer names, and information used by the screen savers.
MSMAIL.INI	Name of workgroup files, personal mail file, and mail-program customization settings.
PROGMAN.INI	Names of the active program manager groups and appearance-related settings for the Program Manager.
PROTOCOL.INI	Settings related to network protocols and hardware drivers.
SCHDPLUS.INI	User name, name of your scheduler file, and other Schedule+ settings.
SHARED.INI	Shared mail system custom commands and messages.
SYSTEM.INI	Information about your system's hardware; specifically, which hardware device driver programs to load when Windows starts up.
WIN.INI	The Windows "user preferences" file, containing a wealth of information about your system, printers, ports, personal preferences, and Windows application programs. Some Windows application programs may add information to this file.
WINFILE.INI	Appearance and operation settings for the File Manager program.

All the .INI files are broken up into sections. Each section begins with the section's name enclosed in square brackets. For example, the first section in WIN.INI is the [windows] section. Each item in an .INI file must be placed in its proper section, or it will be ignored by Windows.

You may add comments to any .INI file by beginning the comment line with a semicolon:

```
;this line contains a comment
```

You will find that comments can be very helpful when you're trying to figure out what you did to your WIN.INI file six months ago. If you make a change to one of your .INI files, we strongly recommend that you place a comment in the file to remind yourself what the line does.

Finally, be careful when editing the .INI files, especially SYSTEM.INI. The SYSTEM.INI file contains information that is closely tied to the particular hardware in your system. It is possible to change SYSTEM.INI in a way that will prevent Windows from starting up properly. Always make a backup copy of your .INI files before making any changes. We've found that it's a good idea to keep an "INIFILES" subdirectory, which contains backup copies of all

.INI files. Once a week or so, copy all your .INI files from the \WINDOWS directory into the \WINDOWS\INIFILES directory and you'll always have a recent .INI file to fall back on.

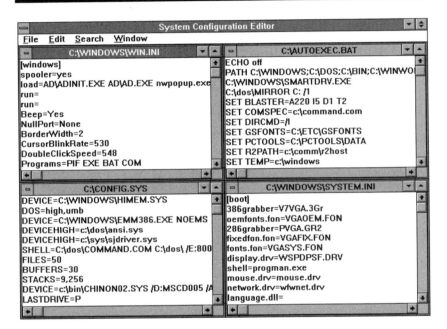

Figure 11.1

The System Configuration Editor program looks and operates much like the familiar Windows Notepad program, but it has the ability to operate on several files at once.

■ Monitoring and Managing Network Activity

If your PC is a Windows for Workgroups server, there may be times when you'll want answers to these questions:

- Who is logged in to my computer?
- Which shared resources are they using?
- Which files do they have open?
- How much of my computer's CPU time is being used to service those users?

Windows for Workgroups includes tools named Net Watcher and WinMeter. These two programs allow you to watch network activity on your PC and measure the amount of CPU time used by network tasks.

Net Watcher

The Net Watcher program shows you who is connected to your computer and which of your shared resources they are using. You can also use the Net Watcher program to disconnect a user from your PC or to close a shared file.

To start the Net Watcher program, double-click on the Net Watcher icon located in the Accessories group. The Net Watcher window appears, as shown in Figure 11.2.

Figure 11.2

This example shows the Net Watcher window display with two users connected to the computer. Both of them are using the same shared disk, as shown in the right column.

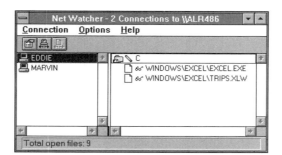

The left window of the Net Watcher display shows who is connected to your computer. The right window shows which of your shared resources are being used. When you click on a user name in the left window, the right window displays the directories, printers, or other shared resources the other person is using and also lists any shared files that person has opened on your PC. A pencil icon next to a resource indicates that the user has write permission, and an eyeglass icon indicates that the user has read-only permission.

To see information on a specific user, select the user's name in the left window and click on the Properties icon; or simply double-click on the user's name. Net Watcher displays the computer name, user name, and other information about the user, as shown in Figure 11.3.

To disconnect a user from your computer, select the user and click on the disconnect icon. To close a file in use by another user, select the file in the right window and click on the close-file icon. Note that these last two actions may cause the remote user to lose his or her work, so you should use them only as a last resort.

WinMeter

WinMeter is a simple program with a single-minded design. It displays a graph showing the amount of CPU time used by application programs running on your PC versus the amount of CPU time used by other users. Figure 11.4 shows a typical WinMeter display.

Figure 11.3

The Net Watcher Properties display shows detailed information about a specific user attached to your computer.

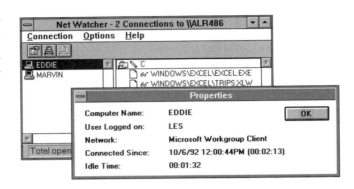

Figure 11.4

This WinMeter display shows how application programs and server duties split the CPU usage on a PC. As server activity increases, the amount of CPU time available for local applications decreases.

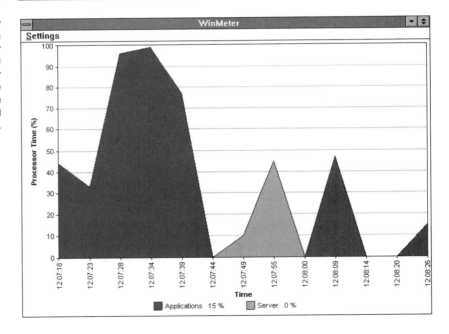

WinMeter can run as a full-screen application program or as an icon. In its iconized form, WinMeter displays a miniature (but very readable) graph. You can adjust the update period of the WinMeter display by selecting the desired update interval from the Settings menu. The available choices are 5 seconds, 15 seconds, 1 minute, 5 minutes (the default), or 15 minutes.

The Always on Top option, which you can select from the Control-menu box, forces WinMeter to remain visible even when other application programs are running. This allows you to monitor network activity while you are working in another application program. If the WinMeter window is too large, you can resize it by clicking and dragging on any corner of the window. Figure 11.5 shows a small WinMeter window on top of Microsoft Word for Windows.

Figure 11.5

You can place a small WinMeter window anyplace on your screen. This allows you to monitor network activity while running another application program. In this example, we're monitoring network activity while editing a file in Microsoft Word for Windows.

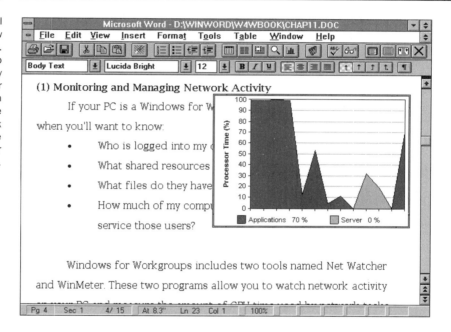

Controlling Server Performance

You can adjust the amount of CPU time devoted to shared resources. If you find that your PC is running slowly because other users are attaching to your PC to use shared resources, adjust the Performance Priority slider bar located in the Network module of the Control Panel, as shown in Figure 11.6.

There are ten "click stops" on the slider; by default, the slider is set on the second position. Moving the bar to the right gives more CPU time to shared resources. Moving it to the left gives more time to local applications. If you're setting up a PC to be used primarily as a server, you may want to move the slider well to the right.

Finding just the right setting may take a few tries; if your PC feels noticeably sluggish, move the slider to the left. If users complain that shared resources on your PC are slow, move the slider to the right.

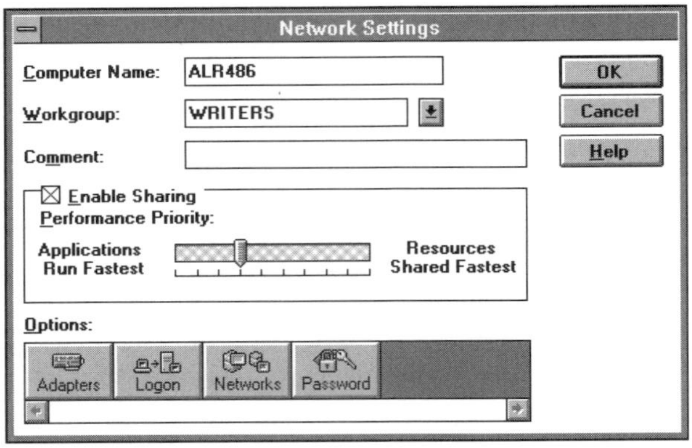

Figure 11.6

By setting the Performance Priority slider bar in the Network module of the Control Panel, you can control how much of your PC's CPU time is devoted to sharing resources.

■ Managing Print Queues

When you print to a shared printer, the application program on your PC sends the print data over the network to the PC that provides the shared print service. Because several users may need to use the same printer at once, the Print Manager program running on the print server places each printer's print data in a holding area called a *print queue*. The Print Manager creates a separate queue for each printer attached to the server PC. When a printer becomes available, the Print Manager begins printing the next job in the print queue. Figure 11.7 shows a typical Print Manager display with several jobs waiting in the print queues.

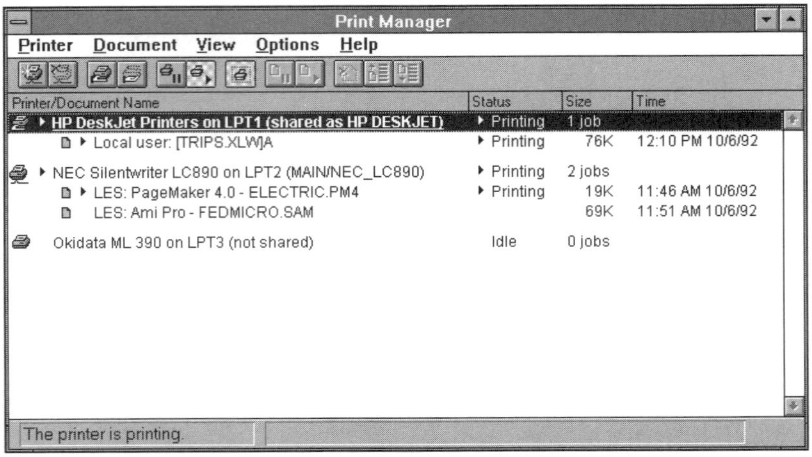

Figure 11.7

The Print Manager display shows the status of each printer, along with a list of jobs that are waiting for it.

You can use the Print Manager to manipulate the jobs that are waiting in the print queue. If you are using a print queue on someone else's PC, you can change only the status of your own print jobs. If you are using a print queue on your own PC, you can manipulate any job in the queue.

To change the order of documents in a queue, click on the icon of the document you want to change and drag it to its new position. Drag it up to make it print sooner or down to make it print later. You can also delete a pending print job by selecting the job and clicking on the delete icon.

■ Defining Additional Printer Ports

Windows for Workgroups supports up to nine printer ports, named LPT1 through LPT9. By default, only the first three ports are defined by the Windows for Workgroups SETUP program. If you need to attach to more than three network printers, you can modify WIN.INI to define up to six additional printer ports.

The three standard LPT1 ports are defined in the [ports] section of WIN.INI. To add additional ports, you must edit WIN.INI and insert the additional port definitions. The following example shows a portion of WIN.INI modified to add two additional ports.

```
[ports]
LPT1:=
LPT2:=
LPT3:=
LPT4:=
LPT5:=
```

■ Restricting Shared Resources

By default, any 386 or 486 PC running Windows for Workgroups may provide shared resources for other users on the network. In some cases, you may wish to prevent specific PCs from being able to share their resources. For example, you may have one PC that contains sensitive payroll or accounting data that should be confined to local access only. Similarly, you may have a printer with blank checks or other preprinted forms that should be accessed only by the PC's local user.

To prevent a PC from providing shared files, follow these steps:

1. Start the File Manager on the PC and make sure that no resources are being shared. If any resources are being shared, select them and click on the Share As icon. Make sure the Re-share at Startup box is not checked.

2. Add these two lines to the WINFILE.INI file:

   ```
   [Restrictions]
   NoShareCommands=1
   ```

   These commands will disable the Share As and Stop Sharing commands in the File Manager's Disk menu.

3. Exit and restart Windows. Start the File Manager and double-check that no resources are being shared and that the Share As and Stop Sharing menu choices do not appear on the Disk menu.

Similarly, you can prevent a PC from providing shared print services by following these steps:

1. Start the Print Manager on the PC and make sure that no print resources are being shared. If necessary, select the shared printer and click on the Share Printer As icon. Make sure the Re-share at Startup box is not checked.

2. Open the WIN.INI file with Notepad or another text editor and search for the section marked [spooler]. Add the following line under the [spooler] heading:

   ```
   NoShareCommands=1
   ```

   This will disable the Share Printer As and Stop Sharing Printer commands in the Print Manager menu.

3. Exit and restart Windows. Start the Print Manager and double-check that no printers are being shared and that the Share Printer As and Stop Sharing Printer menu choices do not appear on the File menu and toolbar.

Use the preceding steps if you want to disable either printer or disk sharing, but not both. To disable all resource sharing, deselect the Enable Sharing check box in the Network module of the Control Panel.

■ Inhibiting the Startup Group

Any programs in the Startup group will automatically load and run when you start Windows for Workgroups. Typical startup programs include screen savers, clock programs, and resource monitor programs.

You can temporarily disable the Startup group when you start Windows for Workgroups. To disable the startup commands, follow one of these steps:

- If your PC has no logon password, hold the Shift key down after you type **WIN** to start Windows for Workgroups. Continue to hold the Shift key until the Program Manager display appears on the screen.

- If your PC has a logon password, press and hold the Shift key after you enter your user name and password when Windows for Workgroups first starts up. Hold the Shift key down until the Program Manager appears on the screen.

■ Managing Persistent Network Connections

As we described in Chapter 4, you can configure Windows for Workgroups to automatically restore network drive and printer connections each time you start Windows for Workgroups. These connections are known as *persistent connections*; they come back each time you start Windows for Workgroups.

Each time you connect a Windows for Workgroups or LAN Manager shared printer or disk, Windows for Workgroups adds the connection information to a file named CONNECT.DAT in your \WINDOWS directory. If you remove a network connection, the connection information is removed from the CONNECT.DAT file.

Because CONNECT.DAT is a stored in encrypted form on your disk, you can't use a text editor to edit or change the entries in the file. You can use the NET USE command to view or delete the persistent-connections list.

To view the persistent connections, type

```
NET USE /PERSISTENT:LIST
```

from the DOS command prompt before you start Windows for Workgroups. To clear the persistent-connections list, type

```
NET USE /PERSISTENT:CLEAR
```

from the DOS prompt. You can also clear the persistent-connections list by deleting the CONNECT.DAT file.

Under NetWare, Windows for Workgroups handles persistent connections differently. Windows for Workgroups and LAN Manager connections are stored in the CONNECT.DAT file, but persistent NetWare connections are stored in the [network] section of WIN.INI. The following example shows a typical [network] section from a WIN.INI file:

```
[Network]
LPT2:=MAIN/NEC_LC890
LPT1:=MAIN/DESKJET
LPT3:=MAIN/OKIDATA
F:=[MAIN/SYS:]
G:=[MAIN/SYS2:]
```

In this example, three printers (LPT1 through LPT3) are connected to NetWare printer queues, and drives F: and G: are connected to network drives SYS: and SYS2:. To change the persistent NetWare connections, you can edit the [network] settings in WIN.INI.

■ Locking Up the Program Manager

If you are installing a Windows for Workgroups PC that will be used by a large number of people, you may want to consider locking up certain Program Manager features. For example, if you are installing a PC for classroom use, you can prevent users from adding or deleting program groups and program icons. This ensures that each student will see the exact same desktop setting when he or she starts Windows for Workgroups.

There are five settings which control the amount of access a user has to the Program Manager File and Options menus. These settings should appear under the [restrictions] heading in the PROGMAN.INI file. By default, none of these settings is included in PROGMAN.INI; if you add one or more, you'll need to add the [restrictions] heading as well.

Table 11.2 lists the five restriction settings and explains their effect on the Program Manager's operation.

■ LAN Manager Visibility

Windows for Workgroups is based on Microsoft's LAN Manager, and the two networks are completely compatible. However, there is one subtle difference that affects interoperation between LAN Manager clients and Windows for Workgroups servers. LAN Manager servers normally announce their presence over the network every few seconds; Windows for Workgroups servers do not. The result is that LAN Manager clients cannot see Windows for Workgroups resources through the LAN Manager NET VIEW command.

To make your Windows for Workgroups PC send the server announcement, add the line

```
LMAnnounce=Ye
```

to the [network] section of SYSTEM.INI. This will enable server broadcasts, and LAN Manager clients will see your PC's name in the LAN Manager browser.

Table 11.2

Available Program Manager Restrictions

ENTRY	PURPOSE
NoRun=	When set to 1, this setting disables the Run command on the File menu. This effectively limits the user to running only those programs that are defined by a Program Manager icon. If NoRun is set to 0, the Run command is enabled.
NoClose=	If NoClose is set to 1, users cannot exit from Windows by using the File menu Exit command, the Control menu Exit command, or Alt+F4. You should enable this setting only if you have another way to exit Windows.
NoSaveSettings=	This setting disables the Save Settings on Exit command on the Options menu. This prevents users from making permanent changes to the appearance of the Program Manager desktop display.
NoFileMenu=	This setting removes the File menu from the Program Manager menu bar. Users can still exit Windows by pressing Alt+F4 or by selecting Exit from the Control menu.
EditLevel=X	EditLevel controls the actions that users can perform in the Program Manager. X must be a number between 0 (no restrictions) and 4 (all restrictions). The restrictions are as follows: X=0 Users may make any changes. X=1 Users may not create, delete, or rename program groups. X=2 All restrictions of X=1. In addition, users may not create or delete program items. X=3 All restrictions of X=2. In addition, users may not modify the program command-line settings in the Properties dialog box. X=4 All restrictions of X=3. In addition, users may not modify any settings in the Properties dialog box.

■ Appendix

■ The Hearts Game: Network Fun!

Windows for Workgroups includes a highly addictive networked version of the Hearts card game. The Hearts game is an interesting example of how people can interact in complex tasks across the network, but it is also a lot of fun to play.

As many as four people can play in a game, and you can have many games going on across the network simultaneously. Figure A.1 shows the window you use to connect to a game.

Figure A.1

The game selection window allows you to find a game getting ready to be played. You can't join a game after the first hand is dealt. You must wait until the players decide to end the game or until one player goes over 100 points.

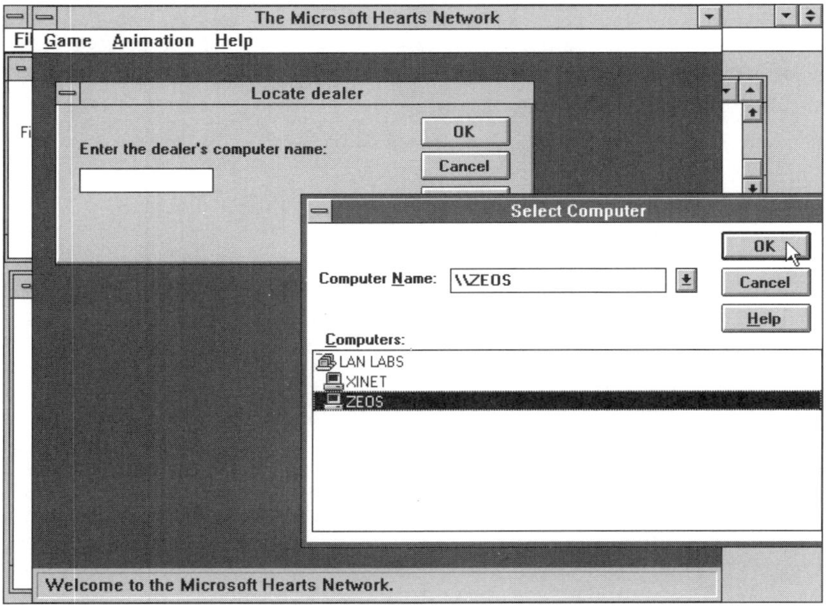

If you don't have four human players to make up a game, the dealer's computer plays the hands of the other players, so you can play alone. The playing table with a hand in progress is shown in Figure A.2.

Figure A.2

The playing table shows only your hand. You use the mouse to select cards to pass and play. During the pass sequence, you can change your mind and withdraw a card by clicking on it again.

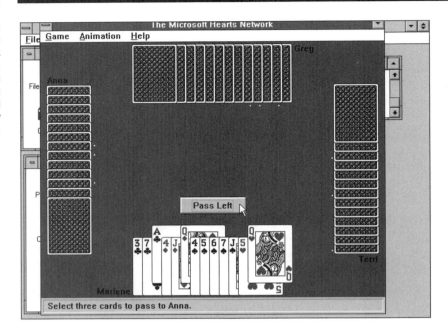

You can change the names of the other players by editing the WIN.INI file. Open WIN.INI with a text editor such as the Windows Notepad, and look for the [Hearts] section. To change the player names, add three lines beneath the [Hearts] heading:

```
p1name=(name)
p2name=(name)
p3name=(name)
```

For example, to set player number one's name to Cindy, you'd enter

```
p1name=Cindy
```

The player name can be up to 14 characters long. See Chapter 11 for detailed information on editing the WIN.INI file.

The instructions for playing Hearts are in the game; we don't intend to teach you the whole game here, but we will explain some strategies you might find interesting.

■ Hearts Hints

In brief, the low score wins. You get points for any card in the heart suit that you take in a trick, and the queen of spades counts 13 points. So the goal of the game is to avoid taking any tricks containing hearts or the queen of spades and to play those cards so that others do take them. However, there is a reverse strategy: If any player takes all the hearts and the queen of spades during the hand, then all the other players get 26 points.

The game allows you to pass three cards when you start each hand. Generally, pass your highest cards, particularly the ace and king of spades. But if you can get rid of an entire suit by passing some midlevel cards, consider doing it. You'll find it useful to play hearts or high spades when someone leads a suit you don't have.

Don't pass any spades below the queen. You might need them if the player passing to you gives you the queen or other high spades.

Don't be afraid to take tricks in the early hands. You can probably lead high cards a few times and take harmless tricks. This technique is a good way to get rid of high cards because you also get some idea of what others are holding. But there is the gamble that someone will slip you the queen of spades if you lead a suit that person isn't holding.

If you take a trick and you have any spades below the queen, play them. See if you can force someone else to play and keep the queen.

Because the game doesn't show you the number of cards the other players have taken in tricks, you must rely on your own memory to warn you if someone is trying to take all the tricks—thereby giving each of the other players 26 points. Watch carefully to see who has taken hearts and the queen of spades in tricks. Don't be so concerned with getting rid of all your hearts that you let another player take all the hearts and the queen.

Be alert to the possibility of taking all the tricks with hearts and the queen of spades yourself. This is a risky strategy, but very satisfying when you pull it off.

■ Glossary

access protocol The traffic rules that LAN workstations abide by to avoid data collisions when sending signals over shared network media; also referred to as the media access control (MAC) protocol. Common examples are carrier sense multiple access (CSMA) and token passing.

address A unique memory location. Network interface cards often use shared memory address locations to move data from the card to the PC's processor.

AFP (AppleTalk File Protocol) Apple's network protocol, used to provide access between file servers and clients in an AppleShare network. Also used by Novell's products for the Macintosh.

AppleTalk An Apple networking system able to transfer data at a rate of 230 kilobytes per second over shielded twisted-pair wire.

ARCnet (Attached Resources Computing Network) A networking architecture (marketed by Datapoint and other vendors) using a token-passing bus architecture, usually on coaxial cable. It is generally implemented in the chips and connectors on the network adapter card.

background program A program that performs its functions while the operator is working with a second, different program.

base address The first address in a series of addresses in memory, often used to describe the beginning of a network interface card's I/O space.

baseband A network that transmits signals as a pulse rather than as variations in a carrier signal.

benchmark A test program used to determine system speed and performance.

boot PROM A read-only memory chip that allows the workstation to communicate with the file server and to read a DOS boot program from the server. Stations can operate on the network without having a disk drive.

broadband A network that carries information riding on carrier waves rather than directly as pulses, providing greater capacity at the cost of higher complexity.

broadcast   To send a message to all stations or an entire class of stations connected to the network.

buffer   A temporary storage space. Data may be stored in a buffer before it is transmitted or as it is received. A buffer may be used to compensate between the differences in the speed of transmission and the speed of processing.

bus topology   A "broadcast" arrangement in which all network stations receive the same message through the cable at the same time.

byte   A group of eight bits.

cache   An amount of RAM set aside to hold data that network stations are likely to access again. The second access, which finds the data in RAM, is very fast.

channel   A path between sender and receiver that carries one stream of information (a two-way path is a circuit).

character   One letter, number, or special code.

client/server computing   A computing system in which processing can be distributed among network "clients" that request information and one or more network "servers" that store data, let clients share data and programs, help with printing operations, and so on. The system accommodates stand-alone applications (such as word processors), applications that require data from the server (such as spreadsheets), applications that use server capabilities to exchange information among users (as with electronic mail), and applications that provide true client/server teamwork (such as databases—especially those based on Structured Query Language, or SQL). Without client/server capabilities, a server downloads an entire database to a client machine for processing; SQL database applications divide the work, allowing the database to stay on the server.

coax or coaxial cable   A type of network media. Coaxial cable contains a copper inner conductor surrounded by plastic insulation and then a woven copper or foil shield. It is commonly used to carry radio-frequency signals, such as those used in cable television and Ethernet networks.

CPU (central processing unit)   The functional "brain" of a computer. The element that does the actual adding and subtracting of 0s and 1s that is essential to computing.

crosstalk   The spillover of a signal from one channel to another, which is very disruptive. Usually, careful adjustment of the circuits will eliminate crosstalk.

CSMA (carrier sense multiple access) A media-sharing scheme in which stations listen in to what's happening on the network media; if the cable is not in use, the station is permitted to transmit its message. CSMA is often combined with a means of performing collision detection, hence CSMA/CD.

cursor The marker indicating the place on the video screen where the next character will appear.

driver A program that interfaces between portions of the LAN software and the hardware on the network interface card.

EISA (Extended Industry Standard Architecture) A PC bus system that is an alternative to IBM's Micro Channel Architecture (MCA). The EISA architecture, backed by an industry consortium headed by Compaq, is compatible with the IBM AT bus; MCA is not.

Ethernet A network cable and access protocol scheme originally developed by Xerox, but now marketed by many companies, including Artisoft.

fiber optics A data transmission method that uses light pulses sent over glass cables.

file server A type of server that holds files in private and shared subdirectories for LAN users. See also *server*.

gateway A shared portal from a local area network into a larger information resource such as a large packet-switched information network or a mainframe computer.

IEEE 802 A set of standards for the physical and electrical connections for local area networks, developed by the IEEE (Institute of Electrical and Electronic Engineers).

IEEE 802.3 10BaseT An evolving IEEE standard describing 10-megabyte-per-second twisted-pair Ethernet wiring. This wiring requires a wiring hub and is useful for installing network monitoring and control devices.

interrupt A signal that suspends a program temporarily, transferring control to the operating system when input or output is required. Interrupts have priority levels, and higher priority interrupts take precedence in processing.

I/O Input-output.

IPX (Internet Packet Exchange) NetWare's native transport protocol, used to move data between server and/or workstation programs running on different network nodes. IPX packets are not related to packets used in Ethernet and similar systems, or to the tokens used in Token-Ring.

IRQ (interrupt request) A computer instruction that interrupts a program for an I/O task. It often is executed through specifically channeled electrical circuits.

jumper A plastic-and-metal shorting bar that slides over two or more electrical contacts to set certain conditions.

K Abbreviation for kilo, meaning 1,000; for example, a 1.2-kbps circuit operates at 1,200 bits per second. When used as a measurement of memory, one K equals 1,024 bytes.

LAN Manager A multiuser network operating system developed jointly by Microsoft and 3Com Corp. LAN Manager provides a wide range of network management and control capabilities.

local Accessed directly in the user's own machine rather than through the network.

local area network (LAN) Connected computers in the same building.

LocalTalk The 230.4-kilobit-per-second media-access method developed by Apple Computer, Inc., for use with its Macintosh computer.

locking A method of protecting shared data. When an application program opens a file, file locking either prevents simultaneous access by a second program or limits such access to read only. DOS versions 3.0 and later allow an application to lock a range of bytes in a file for various purposes. Since DBMS programs interpret this range of bytes as a record, this is called record locking.

MCA (Micro Channel Architecture) The basis for the IBM MicroChannel bus used in high-end models of IBM's PS/2 series of personal computers.

media The cabling or wiring used to carry network signals. Typical examples are coax, fiber-optic, and twisted-pair wire. Plural of medium.

modem (modulator-demodulator) A device that translates between electrical signals and some other means of signaling. Typically, a modem translates between direct-current signals from a computer or terminal and analog signals sent over telephone lines. Other modems handle radio frequencies and light waves.

NDIS (Network Device Interface Specification) A device driver specification developed by Microsoft and 3Com Corp. NDIS provides hardware and protocol independence for network drivers and allows several network protocols to share the same physical network adapter.

NetBEUI (NetBIOS Extended User Interface) A networking protocol designed for use on LANs of 20 to 200 workstations. An extension of NetBIOS, NetBEUI was first introduced by IBM in 1985 and is the primary protocol used by Windows for Workgroups.

NetBIOS (Network Basic Input/Output System) A layer of software originally developed by IBM and Sytek to link a network operating system with specific hardware. It also can open communications between workstations on a network at the session layer. Today, many vendors either provide a version of NetBIOS to interface with their hardware or emulate its session-layer communications services in their network products.

NetWare A series of network operating systems and related products made by Novell, Inc.

network A continuing connection between two or more computers that facilitates the sharing of files and resources.

ODI (Open Data-Link Interface) A standard interface for transport protocols, allowing them to share a single network card without any conflicts.

on-line Connected to a network or host computer system.

Open Systems Interconnection (OSI) reference model A model for networks developed by the International Standards Organization, dividing the network functions into seven connected layers. Each layer builds on the services provided by those under it.

OS/2 (Operating System/2) An operating system developed by IBM and Microsoft for use with Intel's 80286 and 80386 microprocessors. Unlike its predecessor, DOS, OS/2 is a multitasking operating system.

peer-to-peer resource sharing A software architecture that lets any station contribute resources to the network while still running local application programs.

print server A computer on the network that makes one or more attached printers available to other users. The server usually requires a hard disk to spool the print jobs while they wait in a queue for the printer.

print spooler   The software that sends a file to a shared printer over a network, even when the printer is busy. The file is saved in temporary storage and then printed when the printer becomes available.

protocol   A specification that describes the rules and procedures products should follow to perform activities on a network, such as transmitting data. Protocols allow products from different vendors to communicate on the same network.

queue   A list formed by items waiting for service in a system. An example is a print queue of documents to be printed in an electronic publishing system.

record locking   The exclusion of other users from accessing (or sometimes just writing to) a record in a file while a first user is accessing that record.

redirector   A software module that is loaded into every network workstation. It captures application programs' requests for file- and equipment-sharing services and routes them through the network.

RF (radio frequency)   A generic term referring to the technology used in radio, television, cable, and broadband networks. It uses electromagnetic waveforms, usually in the megahertz (MHz) range, for transmission.

ring   A network connection method that routes messages through each station on the network in turn. Most ring networks use a token-passing protocol, which allows the station to put a message on the network when it receives a special bit pattern.

server   Any network computer that makes file, print, or communications services available to other network stations.

serial port   An I/O port that transmits data out one bit at a time, in contrast to a parallel port, which transmits multiple (usually eight) bits simultaneously. RS-232-C is a common serial signaling protocol.

SMB (Server Message Block)   A distributed file system network protocol that allows one computer to use the files and peripherals of another. Originally developed by Microsoft, SMB has been adopted by IBM and other network vendors. SMB is the underlying network protocol used by Microsoft LAN Manager and Windows for Workgroups.

star topology   A network connection method that brings all links to a central node.

T-connector A coaxial connector, shaped like a T, that connects two thin Ethernet cables and has an additional connector for a network interface card.

terminator A resistor used at both ends of an Ethernet cable to ensure that signals do not reflect back and cause errors. It is usually attached to an electrical ground at one end.

thick Ethernet A cabling system that uses large-diameter, stiff cable to connect transceivers. The transceivers connect to the nodes through flexible multiwire cable. Thick Ethernet is also widely known as FYGH cable: frozen yellow garden hose.

thin Ethernet A cabling system that uses a thin, flexible coaxial cable to connect each node to the next node in line.

token passing An access protocol in which a special message (token) circulates among the network nodes, giving them permission to transmit.

Token-Ring The wire and the access protocol scheme whereby stations relay packets around in a logical ring configuration. This architecture is described in the IEEE 802.3 standards.

topology The map of the network. The physical topology describes how the wires or cables are laid out, and the logical or electrical topology describes how the messages flow.

twisted pair Ethernet See *IEEE 802.3 10BaseT.*

twisted-pair wiring Cable composed of two wires twisted together at six turns per inch to provide electrical self-shielding. Some telephone wire—but not all—is twisted-pair.

wiring hub A cabinet, usually mounted in a wiring closet, that holds connection modules for various kinds of cabling. The hub contains electronic circuits that retime and repeat the signals on the cable. The hub may also contain a microprocessor board that monitors and reports network activity.

■ Index

(), 174
* drive specification, 179
;, 185
[], 174
{}, 174

A

access privileges
    for Schedule+, 91–92
    setting in Schedule+, 97–98
    and shared disks, 49
access servers, 147–148
    for remote clients, 155
Access Type box, 53
active printer, 54, 56
adapters and cabling, 22–25
Add to Schedule button in Schedule+, 90
adding
    drive mappings to NetWare, 110, 111
    Macintoshes to PC networks, 116–117
add-on Macintosh connectivity, 116
Address Book, 72–73
administrators and remote-control systems, 157
alias names and e-mail, 68
all-network installation, 39
Alt key combinations
    option for in Workgroup Connection, 167, 169, 170
    for Print Queue screen, 172–173
Ami Pro, installing, 133–134
API (Application Program Interface), 6, 64
Apple SuperDrive, 115–116
AppleTalk, 200
    and sharing printers, 118
Application Program Interface (API), 6, 64
application programs, running via remote control, 148
applications
    installing on servers, 126–127
    installing Word 2.0 and Excel 4.0, 130–132
    single copy per workstation, 124

appointment calendars for Schedule+, 86
Appointments menu in Schedule+, 92
archiving messages, 78–79
ARCnet (Attached Resources Computing Network), 22, 200
ASCII text, importing with e-mail, 75
A:\SETUP, using for Word 2.0 and Excel 4.0, 130–132
asterisk (*) drive specification, 179
ATs
    and DMA channels, 38
    and IRQ2, 37
Attach button, 75, 111
    and NetWare printers, 113
Attached Resources Computing Network (ARCnet), 22, 200
attenuation, 24
AUTOEXEC.BAT, 130
    backing up, 39, 41
    and installing applications, 9, 127
    modifying during installation, 41–42, 43
    and NetWare installation, 105
    and troubleshooting, 43
    and virus control, 29
    and Workgroup Connection, 164, 166
automatic backup and SETUP, 41
automatic installation, 8–10
automation and forms, 5–6
Auto-Pick command in Schedule+, 91

B

backup, 29–30
    and directory structure, 28
    using SETUP for, 41
.BAT file type, 174
batch files, creating with command lines, 174
Bernoulli backup units, 29, 43
binary files, attaching, 75
board settings, changing, 37
boot ROM and network boards, 36
broadcast messages, receiving from NetWare, 107

208 Index

Browse feature in NetWare, 111
browsing, 12
Buffer Size setting for NetWare, 108
buffers and file handles, 42
busy bar, clicking on in Schedule+, 97
buttons
    Address (e-mail), 72
    Add to Schedule, 90
    Attach, 75, 111
    Attach and NetWare printers, 113
    Map in NetWare, 111
    Move (Mail), 79
    NetWare, 110
    Network, 113
    Re-Share at Startup, 58
    Send, 77
    Send Mail, 74
    Server Installation, 130
    Set Root, 112

C

cabling and adapters, 22–25
cache programs, troubleshooting, 43
calendars, importing with Schedule+, 89
carrier sense multiple access (CSMA), 200, 202
centralized administration and server-based networks, 103
changing drive mappings in NetWare, 110
Chat program, 60
CLEAR setting for /PERSISTENT option in NET, 180
client workstations, 104
ClipBook
    activating, 141
    making data objects available with, 13
    using with macros, 7–8
ClipBook server and Viewer, 139
clock, synchronizing in NET, 179
coaxial cable, 22–23
    installing, 25
COM ports and printers, 27
COM2 and IRQ3, 37
command-line interface, 173–174
commands
    adding automatically with SETUP, 42
    Auto-Pick (Schedule+), 91
    Connect, 143
    disabling Share Printer As, 192
    Print Setup, 132
    XCOPY, 126
Comment option, 53
comments, adding to .INI files, 185. *See also* .INIs
communications programs, addressing modems across a LAN with, 159
Compose icon (e-mail), 72
compression
    and PPP, 156
    troubleshooting programs, 43
computer clock, synchronizing in NET, 179
Computer Name option for Workgroup Connection, 167
CONFIG.SYS
    backing up, 39, 41
    commands, 42
    and installing applications, 9, 127
    modifying during installation, 41–42, 43
    and NetWare installation, 105
    and troubleshooting, 43
    and Workgroup Connection, 164
configuration
    reports, 20
    searching files, 136
Connect command, 143
CONNECT.DAT file, 193
connecting to NetWare server from DOS client, 109
connecting PCs and Macintoshes, 116–117
connections, reconnecting in NET, 175
Connect Network Drive icon, 49, 110
Connect Network Printer icon, 56, 114
CONTROL.INI, 185. *See also* .INIs
controlling PCs remotely, 18
Control Panel
    connecting network printer from, 55–56
    connecting printer from, 113–114
    specifying NetWare options from, 106
copper cable systems, 24
copying
    subdirectories, 126
    text and graphics, 138
CPUs
    and communication with network board, 36
    measuring time for, 187–189, 190

Index

sending signals to, 37
creating a Postoffice, 67
crosstalk, 24
Crosstalk, 138
CSMA (carrier sense multiple access), 200, 202
Ctrl key, using to sort messages, 80
C2 security rating, 4–5
cursor
    movement in NET, 171
    repositioning with the mouse, 73
Customize Toolbar, 74
customized software and remote-control systems, 158
cutting, text and graphics, 138

D

Data Drives display in NetWare, 111
data files, multiuser access of, 128
data security and floppy drives, 125
DDE (Dynamic Data Exchange), 6–8, 137
    and LANtastic, 10–11
DDEML (Dynamic Data Exchange Management Library), 138
dedicated access servers, 149
defaults
    for networking scheme, 11
    for printers, 56
    for shared folders, 80
    for Workgroup Connection directories, 165
/DELETE option in NET, 177, 180
deleting drive mappings from NetWare, 111
Depends on Password field, 53
device= commands in CONFIG.SYS, 42
device drivers and SETUP, 41
DEVICE= statement and installation, 9
dial-out products, 160
Direct Memory Access (DMA)
    channels and installation, 34
    using to speed data transfer, 38
directories
    defaults for, 165
    navigating in NetWare, 109
    structures for servers, 28
Disconnect icon, 50
disconnecting users, 187
Disk Connections menu in NET, 168, 170
diskless workstations and installation, 39
disks
    connecting and disconnecting with NET, 168, 169–170
    disconnecting in NET, 180
    sharing, 48
    space requirements for, 38–39
    troubleshooting cache programs, 43
    troubleshooting disk-compression programs, 43
display systems and graphical objects, 76
.DLLs
    drivers and remote-control systems, 150
    and installing files, 130
DMA (Direct Memory Access)
    channels and installation, 34
    using to speed data transfer, 38
DOS
    accepting commands from command line in NET, 173–174
    connecting clients with NetWare server, 109
    file types, 117–118
    path name option for in Workgroup Connection, 167
    and peer-to-peer networks, 102
    requirements for running Workgroup Connection, 164
    running WordPerfect for Windows from prompt, 135
drivers
    installing for NetWare, 105, 106
    for printers, 54–55
    selecting for Workgroup Connection, 167
drives
    adding and removing for NetWare, 110–112
    changing letters in NET, 169
    handling mappings with NetWare, 107
dynamic data exchange (DDE), 6–8, 137
    and LANtastic, 10–11
dynamic data exchange management library (DDEML), 138

E

EDIT.EXE, 174
editing files, 184, 185
editing notes, inserting with Ami Pro, 133

EditLevel=X Program Manager
   restriction, 195
8514 video adapter, 43
EISA (Extended Industry Standard
   Architecture), 36, 202
e-mail concept, 65–66
embedded objects, 140
EMM386, 41, 43
environment files for WordPerfect for
   Windows, 135
error messages. *See also* .INIs
   disabling in NetWare, 108
   and NET HELP, 175
   and WIN.INI, 122
Ethernet, 22
   installing adapters to Macintoshes, 116–117
   10BaseT, 22, 23
etiquette, 61
Excel 4.0, installing, 130–132
.EXE files and remote-node operations, 152
exiting from Windows, 61
   preventing, 195
expansion slots, problems with, 36
Extended Industry Standard Architecture
   (EISA), 36, 202
extended memory and NetWare drivers, 9

F

F: drive, 48
fiber-optic cabling, 24
fields, moving between in e-mail, 73
file handles and buffers, 42
FILE HANDLES= command in
   NetWare, 109
File menu, removing from Program
   Manager, 195
file servers, 25–26
   installing and loading Windows from, 39,
   40–41
   and PCs, 53
   for Postoffice, 66
file transfer feature, 8
files
   closing, 187
   editing, 184
   managing with remote-control systems, 157
   moving on server-based networks, 46
   multiuser access to, 128
   overwriting, 127–128
   types for Macintoshes and DOS, 117–118
Find option in Schedule+, 93, 94
finding messages, 79, 80
floppy drives, exchanging for hard-disk
   drives, 125
folders
   creating for Mail, 79
   sharing, 79–80
forms and automation, 5–6
forms handling concept, 87
Full field, 53

G

games, building interactively, 8
game selection window, 197
Global Resource Visibility, 107
graphical objects, importing with e-mail,
   75–77
graphics
   and remote-node systems, 158
   selecting to link, 140
graphics mode, 169

H

Hang Up icon, 60
hard-disk drives
   and client PCs, 123
   exchanging floppy drives for, 125
hard disks
   installation, 39, 40
   storage and remote-node operations, 151
hardware configuration, 123
hardware interrupts, 26
Hearts, 198
high memory, loading Workgroup
   Connection into, 166
High Performance File System (HPFS), 102
high-speed modems, 153–155
   sharing for dialing out, 158–160
HIMEM.SYS, 38
   installing with SETUP, 41
   and troubleshooting, 43
hot links, 137
HPFS (High Performance File System), 102

I

I/O (input/output), 36–38
icons
    Chat, 60
    Compose (e-mail), 72
    Connect Network Drive, 49, 110
    Connect Network Printer, 56, 114
    Disconnect, 50
    Hang Up, 60
    Inbox, 77
    Mail, 66
    Network and LAN Manager, 114
    open book (e-mail), 72
    pencil, 187
    Print Manager, 61
    Printers, 129
    Private Folders, 77
    Properties, 187
    Schedule+, 87
    Send Mail, 74
    Set Default Printer, 56
    Share, 52
    Share Printer, 57
    Telephone Dial, 60
    using to control security, 29
improving performance, 28
Inbox, 73, 77, 78
incompatible programs and hardware, listing of, 43
Industry Standard Architecture (ISA) bus, 36
information, linking and inserting, 140
Inherited Resource Visibility and NetWare, 107
.INIs, 9, 166. *See also individual .INI file names*
    editing, 184
    and WordPerfect for Windows, 135, 136
initialization files, 184, 185
initializing Mail, 69
input/output (I/O), 36–38
INSTALL
    vs. SETUP, 126
    using with 1-2-3 for Windows and Ami Pro, 133–134
    and WordPerfect for Windows, 135
installing
    Ami Pro, 133–134
    applications on servers, 126–127
    LAN Manager driver, 114–115
    menu for Word 2.0, 131
    methods for, 39–40
    1-2-3 for Windows, 133–134
    PowerPoint 3.0, 132–133
    WordPerfect for Windows, 135–136
    Word 2.0 and Excel 4.0, 130–132
    Workgroup Connection, 167
interactive games, building, 8
internal mouse adapters and PCs, 38
Internet Packet Exchange (IPX), 203. *See also* TSRs
interrupt, 202
    14 and 6BH, 159
    request (IRQ), 9, 37, 203
inventory form, 19
IPX (Internet Packet Exchange), 203. *See also* TSRs
    NetWare TSR, 104
    and Network Warning, 108
    TSR for ODI, 104
IRQs, 9, 37, 155, 203
    addresses and LAN adapters, 35
    scanning for, 20
ISA (Industry Standard Architecture) bus, 36

K

keystrokes and hardware interrupts, 26

L

LAN adapters
    installing, 20
    loading drivers for, 9
    and PCs with mainframe connections, 38
    troubleshooting, 35–36
LAN Manager
    clients vs. Windows for Workgroups servers, 194
    installing driver for, 114–115
    for NT, 5
    and OS/2, 102
LAN Server, 12
LANtastic and DDE, 10–11
laptops
    connecting to networks, 34
    and e-mail, 70
    and remote-node operations, 152
LASTDRIVE statement and installing NetWare, 105–106

212   Index

levels of UL certification, 24
licensing for software, 124
LIM EMS 4.0 standard, 38
line wrapping in e-mail, 75
linking, 139–140
LIST setting for /PERSISTENT option in NET, 180
LMAnnounce=Ye, 194
local drive, redirecting in NET, 179
local hard-disk installation, 39, 40
LocalTalk, 116, 203
    and sharing printers, 118
locking records, 49
logging
    into NetWare, 111
    on and off in NET, 175
logical drives, 48
Login line in MSMAIL.INI, 69. *See also* .INIs
LOGIN for NetWare, 106
login scripts and NetWare, 110
LOGIN.BAT, 174
LOGIN.EXE and NetWare, 112
Lotus Notes, 85
low-DOS memory, 36
low-end networks, 102
LPT ports
    assigning, 129–130
    and printers, 27
    and WordPerfect for Windows, 136
LSL.COM TSR for ODI, 104

M

MAC (media access control) protocol, 22, 200
Macintoshes
    file types for, 117–118
    linking, 12
    and PC programs, 115
macros, linking applications with, 7–8
Mail icon, 66
Mail Options, 71
Mail program, installing for Workgroup Connection, 167
mail and scheduling, 5–6
mailbox names, 68
mainframe connections in PCs, 38
managing networks, 51
Map button in Netware, 111

mappings, inheriting and changing, 107–108
MCA (Micro Channel Architecture), 36, 203
media access control (MAC) protocol, 22, 200
meetings
    notification using Schedule+, 87
    scheduling, 91
memory
    addressing and I/O, 36–37
    and client PCs, 123
    locations of, 35, 200
    for NET, 169
    and NetWare drivers, 9
    for remote-node operations, 151
    requirements for installation, 10, 38, 169
memory-management software, selecting, 18
menus, switching between in NET, 168
menu systems, 28–29
Message Finder, 80
Message Status at Startup group for NetWare, 107
messages
    creating with graphical objects, 76–77
    finding and tracking, 79, 80
    sending, 77
Micro Channel Architecture (MCA), 36, 203
Microsoft
    Diagnostics (MSD.EXE), 20
    Mail 3.0, 5
    Mail Transfer Agent, 5
    Schedule+, 5
    SMB (Server Message Block) protocol, 10, 11
    Word for Windows and Word for the Macintosh, 115
    XMS standard, 38
mixed local/network installation, 39
mixed-platform networks, 115
.MMF files, 70
modems, 153–155
    and COM2, 37
    networking, 158
    remote-control software for, 148
    for RLN, 155
modem server, 158
mouse
    using to reposition the cursor, 73
    using with Schedule+, 94
Move button (Mail), 79

moving
  cursor in NET, 171
  text and graphics, 138
MSD.EXE (Microsoft Diagnostics), 20
MS-DOS and peer-to-peer networks, 102
MSIPX
  in AUTOEXEC.BAT, 106
  command added on NetWare, 42
  and Network Warning, 108
MSMAIL.INI, 69, 185. *See also* .INIs
multiplatform support, and server-based networks, 103
multiple-CPU systems, 150
multiplexing, 150
multitasking, and OS/2, 102
multiuser access, 49

N

named pipes, 167
NASI (Network Asynchronous Server Interface), 159
NDIS (Network Device Interface Specification), 10, 11, 204
near-end crosstalk (NEXT), 24
NET
  commands, displaying summary of, 175
  .EXE, 173
  loading as a TSR, 169
  menus, switching between, 168
  START command, 42
  USE, 179–180
Net Watcher, 187, 188
  and Workgroup Connection, 167
NetBEUI (NetBIOS Extended User Interface), 10, 11, 204
NetBIOS (Network Basic Input/Output System) protocol, 10
  Extended User Interface (NetBEUI), 204
  and NetBEUI, 139
NetWare
  button, 110
  drivers and extended memory, 9
  Map utility, 9
  operating system, 102
  options screen, 106
  as server-based system, 104
  Warning group for NetWare, 108

[network] and .INI files, 193, 194. *See also* .INIs
Network Asynchronous Server Interface (NASI), 159
Network Basic Input/Output System (NetBIOS) protocol, 10
Network Card option for Workgroup Connection, 167
Network Device Interface Specification (NDIS), 10, 11, 204
networks
  administrators and remote-control systems, 157
  boards problems, 36
  button, 113
  configuration display for NET, 174
  and DDE (Dynamic Data Exchange), 6–8
  defaults for adapters, 36
  disk and printer control, 48
  interface cards (NICs) and installation, 34, 35–36
  manager for Mail, 80–81
  managers, 51
  and modem limitations, 159
  monitoring activity on, 188–189
  options for Workgroup Connection, 166
  printer connections from Control Panel, 113–114
  scheme default for, 11
  and security, 29
  sessions, 150
  software configuration, 37
  survey form for, 19
  and traffic, 39
  types of, 46
NETX
  adding command to AUTOEXEC.BAT, 42
  changing command in AUTOEXEC.BAT, 109
  and NetWare TSR, 104
  and Network Warning, 108
  shell program for NetWare, 105
New Recurring Appointments option in Schedule+, 92
NEXT (near-end crosstalk), 24
/NI=, 136
NICs (Network Interface Cards) and installation, 34, 35–36

NoClose= Program Manager restriction, 195
NoFileMenu= Program Manager restriction, 195
nonplenum cable, 24
NoRun= Program Manager restriction, 195
NoSaveSettings= Program Manager restriction, 195
NO setting for /PERSISTENT option in NET, 180
NoShareCommands=1, adding to WINFILE.INI, 192. *See also* .INIs
Notepad program, and e-mail, 74
Notes area of Schedule+, 90
/NT=, 135
NWShare handles, 107

O

object linking and embedding (OLE), 139–140
objects
   in ClipBook, 139
   copying from ClipBook into local Clipboard, 143
   linking, 142–143
   moving to the Clipboard, 140
   pasting from the Clipboard to ClipBook, 141–142
   real-time updates for, 142
   sharing via DDE, 137
ODI (Object Data-Link Interface), 104, 204
OLE (object linking and embedding), 139–140
1-2-3 for Windows, installing, 133–134
open book icon (e-mail), 72
Open Data-Link Interface (ODI), 104, 204
Open Systems Interconnection (OSI), 204
options, changing for Workgroup Connection, 166
options screen for NetWare, 106
OSI (Open Systems Interconnection), 204
OS/2 and LAN Manager, 12, 102
overlay files, 28
overwriting files, 127–128

P

packets, troubleshooting, 156
pages, in ClipBook, 139
Paintbrush and Mail program, 76
password-list file, 180

passwords, 51–52
   changing in NET, 176
   and ClipBook items, 142
   and e-mail, 67
Passwords box, 53
Paste Link option, 144
Paste Special command, 144
pasting, text and graphics, 138
path names, browsing in NET, 170
Path option, 52, 167
Pathworks server, 10, 12
/PAUSE option in NET and printing, 177
PC LAN file server, connecting LocalTalk to, 116
PCs
   controlling remotely, 18
   and DMA2, 38
   as file servers, 53
   and Macintosh programs, 115
   and power consumption, 26
   as servers, 25–26
peer-to-peer networks, 46
pencil icon, 187
Permanent connection of printers, 114
Permanent drive mappings in NetWare, 112
permanent share, 53
persistent NetWare connections, changing, 194
/PERSISTENT option in NET, 180
pictures, inserting in e-mail, 76–77
players, changing names of, 198
playing table, 198
Point-to-Point Protocol (PPP), 156
Pop-Up Key option for Workgroup Connection, 167
pop-up menu for NET, 168–169
portables, connecting to networks, 34
ports
   assigning for printers, 129–130
   defining, 191
   disconnecting in NET, 171
   redirecting for printers in NET, 179
Postoffice and e-mail, 65–66, 67
Postoffices, managing, 80
PostScript printers, sharing between PCs and Macintoshes, 118
power failures, and remote-control programs, 148–149

Index

POWERLan server, 11–12
PowerPoint 3.0, installing, 132–133
PPP (Point-to-Point Protocol), 156
presentations, switching to in Schedule+, 86
previewing printing, 59
print jobs
    checking, 172–173
    deleting, 191
    sending, 59
Print Manager, connecting to network printer from, 56, 57
Print Manager icon, 61
Print option, for Schedule+, 93
print preview, 59
print queues, 172
    changing order of documents in, 191
    displaying and modifying in NET, 177
    managing, 190–191
printer, disconnecting in NET, 180
Printer Connections menu, exiting from, 171
Printer Connections in NET, 168
Printer Connections screen
    exiting from, 172
    switching display to in NET, 171
printer drivers, for WordPerfect for Windows, 136
printer ports, 27
    defining, 191
    redirecting in NET, 179
    and Workgroup Connection, 170
printers
    browsing in NET, 171
    connecting to, 55–57
    connecting from Control Panel, 113–114
    connecting and disconnecting with NET, 168, 170–172
    connecting to when shared, 48
    disconnecting in NET, 172
    installing for 1-2-3 for Windows and Ami Pro, 134
    sharing, 57–58, 129–130
    sharing between PCs and Macintoshes, 118
Printers icon, 129
printing
    controlling with Print Queue, 172–173
    options for in NET, 177
    remotely, 157
Printing group for NetWare, 108
Print Setup command, 132
Private Folders icon, 77
PROGMAN.INI, 185. *See also* .INIs
program files, searching for in WordPerfect for Windows, 136
Program Manager, 194, 195
Properties icon, 187
Protocol Driver option for Workgroup Connection, 167
PROTOCOL.INI, 166, 185. *See also* .INIs
protocols and NetWare installation, 105
/PS=, 136

Q

QEMM and installation, 41
QIC (quarter-inch tape cartridge) backup systems, 29
questionnaire for network requirements, 21
queues and sending messages, 77

R

RAM, 201
    address determination of, 36
    drive as swap drive, 39
    and remote-node operations, 153
RAM requirements, 10
    for file servers, 26
    monitoring, 20
RAS (Remote Access Service), 153, 156–157
reading PC and Macintosh programs, 115
read-only
    access, 128
    field, 53
    permission, 187
real-time updates, 142
reconnecting in NET, 170, 171
record locking, 49
Redirector option for Workgroup Connection, 167
redirector programs, 159
    displaying type and version of in NET, 181
    loading and unloading for NET, 177–178
    starting, 42
reducing network load, 28
regular meetings, scheduling automatically, 92
reliability and server-based networks, 103
Remote Access Service (RAS), 153, 156–157

216 Index

remote computers, 154
remote control, dialing-in using, 148–150
Remote LAN Node (RLN), 155
remote-node operations, requirements for, 151
remote-node systems and printing, 157
remote PCs, loading utilities on, 157
removable hard disks and troubleshooting, 43
Re-Share, 53, 58
resource allocation and NetWare, 107
resource password, 180
resources, location of, 8
[Restrictions], 192, 194
/RESUME option in NET, and printing, 177
RLN (Remote LAN Node), 155
ROM and network boards, 36
root drive mappings for NetWare, 112
Run command, disabling, 195
running NET, 168

S

safety standards for cabling, 23–24
SAVE setting for /PERSISTENT option in NET, 180
Save Settings, disabling, 195
SCHDPLUS.INI, 185. *See also* .INIs
Schedule+ icon, 87
scheduling and mail, 5–6
SCSI disk controllers, 38
searching
 for program files in WordPerfect for Windows, 136
 in Schedule+, 93, 94
security, 29, 51
 and directory structure, 28, 29
 and file servers, 26–27
 and floppy drives, 125
 and remote control, 149
 and server-based networks, 103
 and Windows NT, 4–5
Send button, 77
Send Mail icon and button, 74
serial communications, 159
serial mouse and COM2, 37
serial ports, 205
 redirecting traffic through, 154
\\server, 179
server-based networks, 46, 47, 103

Server Installation button, 130
Server Message Block (SMB) protocol, 10, 11, 205
server volume in NetWare, 111
Serverpath line in MSMAIL.INI, 69. *See also* .INIs
servers, 10–12
 controlling performance of, 189
 directory structure for, 28
 displaying shared resources on in NET, 181
 and NetWare, 104
 requirements for, 25–27
 selecting in NET, 170, 171
 sending announcements on, 194
Set Access Privileges option in Schedule+, 97
Set As Default Printer, 56
Set Default Printer icon, 56
/SET option in NET, 179
Set Root button, 112
setting access privileges in Schedule+, 97
settings for NetWare, 106–107
SETUP, 40, 41, 125
 .EXE and NetWare drivers, 105
 vs. INSTALL, 126
 for PowerPoint 3.0, 132–133
 and printer ports, 191
 and printer selection, 54
 troubleshooting, 42–43
 .TXT file, 43
 for Word 2.0 and Excel 4.0, 130–132
 for Workgroup Connection, 164–166, 167
Share As command, disabling, 192
Share Directory, 52–53
Share icon, 52
Share Name option, 52
Share Printer As command, disabling, 192
Share Printer icon, 57
shared data, protecting, 203
shared disks
 connecting to, 48, 49–50
 selecting in NET, 170
 setting up, 52–53
shared folders, compressing, 81
SHARED.INI, 185. *See also* .INIs
shared printers
 browsing in NET, 171
 connecting to, 55–57

Index

shared resources
    disconnecting in NET, 175
    displaying with NET, 180
    identifying, 187
    restricting, 191–192
    scheduling with Schedule+, 87
shared-session access servers, 150
shared storage for e-mail, 67
shared subdirectories and e-mail, 68
sharing drives, 8
sharing PostScript printers between PCs and Macintoshes, 118
SHELL.CFG configuration file for NetWare, 108–109
shell program for NetWare, 105
SHOW DOTS= command in NetWare, 109
signaling
    for RLN, 155
    speeds for, 153
signals, spilling over of, 201
SMARTRV.EXE, 43
SMB (Server Message Block) protocol, 10, 11, 205
software, customized, 158
software licensing, 124
sorting messages, 78, 80
speed
    of data transfer, 38
    increasing via remote control, 148
    requirement for RLN, 155
    of root-drive scans in NetWare, 112
spooler, 192
spooling, 172
spreadsheets
    installing Excel 4.0, 130–132
    installing 1-2-3 for Windows, 133–134
    and linking, 140
SQL (Structured Query Language), 201
STACKER, 43
Standard mode, 48
standards for cabling, 23
Startup group, inhibiting, 192–193
Startup option for Workgroup Connection, 167
star wiring configuration, 23
Stop Sharing commands, disabling, 192
storage on e-mail, 66
Structured Query Language (SQL), 201

subdirectories
    copying, 126
    structures of, 28
Subject field in e-mail, 73
SuperDrive, 115–116
survey form, 19
SyDOS, 43
    cartridges for, 29
symmetrical multiprocessing and Windows NT, 5
SyQuest cartridges, 29
System Configuration Editor, 184, 186
SYSTEM.INI, 185. *See also* .INIs
    modifying, 43
System Sleuth, 20

T

Tab key, using to move between fields in e-mail, 73
tape-drive controllers and PCs, 38
task manager for Schedule+, 89–90
tasks
    managing with Schedule+, 94
    sharing, 137
TCP/IP network drivers and Windows NT, 5
telecommuting, 148
Telephone Dial icon, 60
telephone lines, costs of, 158
temporary share, 53
10BaseT (Ethernet), 22, 23, 26
10NET server, 11, 12
terminate-and-stay-resident programs. *See* TSR
text
    editing, 135
    editors, 174, 184
    importing and exporting with Ami Pro, 133
    processor for e-mail, 75
    selecting to link, 140
    using with games, 198
thin net wiring, 22–23
32-bit code, 4
3Com 3+ Open, selecting in WordPerfect for Windows, 135
386 Enhanced group for NetWare, 107
386-Enhanced mode, 48
386Max and installation, 41

tips for managing remote nodes, 157
to-do lists, creating in Schedule+, 90
tokenizing
    and PPP, 156
    and Shiva, 154
Token-Ring, 22
Toolbar icons, 9
tracking messages, 79, 80
traffic rules, 200
training, 30
troubleshooters and remote-control systems, 157
troubleshooting
    LAN adapter problems, 35–36, 38
    SETUP program, 42–43
TSR (terminate-and-stay-resident). *See also* IPX (Internet Packet Exchange)
    loading NET as, 169
    for NetWare, 104
    and scheduling, 85

U

UL (Underwriters Laboratory) safety standards, 23–24
uninterruptable power supply (UPS), 26
unshielded twisted-pair wire, installing, 24–25
Update Seconds setting for NetWare, 108
UPS (Uninterruptable Power Supply), 26
usage information for NET commands, 174–181
User Name option for Workgroup Connection, 167
user names
    and e-mail, 67
    reading, 5
    in Schedule+, 87, 88
users
    adding in Schedule+, 97–98
    calling with Chat, 60
    controlling actions of, 195
    identifying, 187
utilities, loading on remote nodes, 157

V

VA (volt/amps) and UPS systems, 26
VGA video adapters, 43
video adapters
    and graphical objects, 76
    memory requirements for, 18
video boards and installation, 43
viewing drive mappings in NetWare, 110
views, switching to in Schedule+, 86
virtual circuit, 158
virtual machines and NetWare, 107
viruses
    and floppy drives, 125
    protection programs and running SETUP, 43
    and security, 29
volt/amps (VA) and UPS systems, 26

W

warning message, overriding in NET, 175, 178
wattage ratings, 26
Windows
    applications and remote systems, 158
    exiting from, 61
    family relationships in, 4
    master copy and installation, 40–41
    Notepad, 135
    NT (New Technology), 3–5
WINDOWS\SYSTEM subdirectory, 130
Windows for Workgroups servers vs. LAN Manager clients, 194
WINFILE.INI, 74, 185. *See also* .INIs
WIN.INI, 122, 126, 130, 184, 185. *See also* .INIs
    and installation, 9
    modifying, 43
WinMeter, 187–189
WIN32 SDK (System Developer's Kit), 4
wiring and adapters, 22–25
Word for the Macintosh and Microsoft Word, 115
word processors and linking, 140
WordPerfect for Windows, installing, 135–136
Word 2.0, installing, 130–132
Workgroup Connection
    limitations of, 164
    loading redirector software for, 177–178
WORKGROUP:groupname, 179
Workgroup Name option for Workgroup Connection, 167
workstations, 104
/WPC= in WP.ENV file, 136

WPGO, 67
write permission, 187
WSGEN for NetWare customization, 104

X

XCOPY command, 126
X: drive, 48
XTs, and DMA channels, 38

Y

Y connector for the Macintosh, 116
YES setting for /PERSISTENT option in
    NET, 180
/Y option in NET, 176